Depression is a Liar

It is possible to recover and be happy again – even

if you don't believe it right now

By Danny Baker

CONTENTS

DEPRESSION IS A LIAR... 6

I WILL NOT KILL MYSELF, OLIVIA........................... 197

PROLOGUE

I picked up the sharpest piece of glass I could find on the side of the road and put it to my throat.

'No!' someone screamed, running towards me.

'Stay back!' I yelled, holding out the glass.

The man froze, raising his hands in the surrender sign.

'Pl-please ...' he stuttered. 'Please don't do this. Whatever happened ... it can be fixed.'

'What the fuck do you know?' I yelled. 'You don't know what it's like to be me! You're not crazy! You don't want to kill yourself one week and chase hallucinations the next! What the fuck do you know? What the *fuck* do you know?'

'OK, OK,' he motioned, patting the air. 'I'm sorry. Just please don't do this. *Please.*'

The crowd all tried to talk me into dropping the glass, but once again I brought it to my neck. I pierced the skin, felt hot blood dripping onto my hand.

Death. I craved it, craved it.

It was like a maddening hunger that I wanted to feed so badly. Everything was just so fucked up. Everything had been fucked up for so long and I was sure that this was the only way out. There was nothing I wanted to do but satisfy that craving. Nothing I wanted to do but die. Running that piece of glass over my throat made me feel better, thinking that the craving's about to be fed, thinking that the pain's about to end. So close to the apathy of death. Nothingness! The end! An escape at last!

Plunge it through your throat! Through your fucking throat! Now! Now!

My hand trembled wildly. My whole body shook.

Do it! Kill yourself! End it now!

My hand kept trembling and trembling before finally, the glass slipped through my fingers and fell to the ground. I couldn't do it. I exploded into tears, cried loudly as all my emotions ruptured inside me – in large part because I knew I'd have to keep living and fighting in this crazy fucked up world – but regardless, I knew I couldn't do it. I'm just not a quitter. When it really comes down to it I'm just not a quitter.

A couple of people helped me to my feet, moved me away from the wreckage. I sat hugging my shins on the sidewalk, crying with my head buried in my knees as the crowd watched on silently.

'You're not a quitter,' I kept sobbing to myself. 'You're not a quitter.'

The police arrived. They asked me what happened.

'You're not a quitter,' I kept repeating.

'So fix this.'

Taking a deep breath, I did my best to gather myself before looking up at the officers. And then I told them what happened.

'I'll plead guilty to whatever offence you see fit to charge me with,' I said when I had finished. 'But first, I need to be admitted to a psych ward.'

*

The above excerpt is actually the prologue of my as yet unpublished novel *I Will Not Kill Myself, Olivia.*

'What's your book about?' everyone would ask me while I was writing it.

An informative answer might've been that it is a tale of lost innocence, of a boy-going-on-man being sucked so deep into the vortex of depression that he self-destructs almost to the point of death; that it is a book about breakages – both psychological and romantic – yet also one about second chances; and that above all else, it is the story of Jimmy, of Olivia, and of the love that binds them.

But at the time, I didn't want to be informative.

'It's just a messy love story,' I'd mutter before quickly changing the subject.

My novel wasn't something I liked talking about because while I was working on it, I was afraid of being asked the inevitable question:

'What gave you the idea to write about mental illness?'

I don't like lying, and that wasn't a question I was comfortable answering honestly. I wasn't ready to tell anyone that I was just writing what I know – that while my protagonist Jimmy is his own character in his own world, that the apple, so to speak, did not fall far from the tree. I wasn't ready to tell anyone that the only reason I could write authentically about depression – and the alcoholism, drug abuse, medicine-induced psychosis, near-suicide attempts and hospitalisations it can lead to – was because I'd experienced it all myself. I was still in the thick of it. Still trying to get better. I didn't want anyone but the people closest to me knowing what I was going through.

I was gradually able to recover, however, and by the time I'd finished my novel at the end of 2012, I was happy, and ready to be open about my plight to try and help others who were suffering like I had. At the same time I was starting to think about finding a publisher, and that's when I came up with the Depression Is Not Destiny Campaign, to inspire victims of the illness to never give up on happiness. It centres around a video blog following my quest to get *I Will Not Kill Myself, Olivia* published, which will hopefully culminate in the moment when I am offered a contract. Through my blog and this memoir I want everyone to know what I went through, to understand how I recovered, and to be there with me when I hopefully achieve my dream of becoming a published author; if and when it happens, I want everyone to see how overwhelmingly happy I'll be, I want everyone to literally see the tears of joy streaming down my cheeks, because it will show them that depression is beatable, and that even the most severely afflicted can overcome it and go on to live happy, healthy, fulfilling lives. I think seeing me come full-circle – from on the brink of suicide to achieving my dream – will give others hope that they can do the same.

So with that in mind, this is my story – told as candidly as I can possible write it. I hope that after reading it, you'll understand why I'll be so emotional if and when my novel gets published, and I hope you'll be there with me in that wonderful moment of bliss.

PART I:

WARNING SIGNS

OR

I DID NOT *RAPE* HER!

At the annual Sydney University Scholarship Dinner I got talking to Mr Williams, one of my old high school teachers who'd been invited by my faculty.

'So how've you been, Danny?' Mr Williams asked.

'Top of the world, Mr W! I'm really happy to be studying Commerce/Law, and I've also started writing my first novel called *Chrysalis* about an orphan's plight in the Great Depression of the 1930's. This year's going to be great! I'm going to get a High Distinction average across all of my subjects, and have my novel published by the end of the year! And when I finish my degree, I'm going to become a rich investment banker or a management consultant, and travel all over the world and live up the high life! It's going to be incredible! I can't wait to jump right into it!'

I kept talking, giddy with excitement as Mr Williams listened indulgently. At some point the mains were served, after which, each scholarship holder was called up on stage and presented with an award.

'Congratulations, Danny,' Mr Williams said back at our table. 'You did really well to get such a coveted scholarship. I know you worked hard for it, and you deserve it as much as anyone.'

'Thanks,' I smiled.

'You've been blessed with so much,' he continued. 'You've been brought up in a wonderful neighbourhood; you're surrounded by a loving, supportive family; and you've got the opportunity and the ability to do anything you want to in life.'

He paused for a moment.

'I hope you use your blessings for good,' he said. 'I hope you always do charity work, and I hope you always try to help people.'

He paused again.

'Remember, Danny: to whom much is given, much is expected.'

As you can see, I started off college feeling exuberant, confident, hopeful and joyous. The future seemed full of promise and wonder, and if you'd told me that soon I would hate my life and wish I was dead, I would've thought you were crazy. But, like so many illnesses, depression is one we often think will never befall us. Particularly when times are good, we often think we're immune to it – even though given the wrong confluence of factors, it can crush absolutely anybody.

In my case, my deterioration began when to my great dismay, my first semester of uni turned out to be a whole lot harder than I'd thought. Whenever I studied as much as I needed to to get a High Distinction average, I barely got any writing done; and whenever I stuck to writing – which was most of the time because I loved it so much – I fell behind at uni. Considering that in addition to studying full-time and writing my first novel, I was also playing on the university basketball team, tutoring high school students to earn some money, and going out partying twice a week, there was a lot on my plate – but being the perfectionist I was, I was never going to use that as an excuse for not achieving my goals. Consequently, I felt disgusted with myself for being behind in my subjects, and furious with myself for not working harder.

But thank God the exams are still a few weeks away! I remember thinking. *So, if I drink lots of caffeine and pull some all-nighters, I should be able to catch up and still get my High Distinction average.*

Fucking hell! I swore when I got my exam marks back. *Fuck me dead! An average of 74%! That's fucking terrible! That's eleven-fucking-percent off a High Distinction average! What a disgrace. What an embarrassment. I fucked up this semester. I failed.*

Once again, I felt so angry, so appalled with myself for not working harder and achieving my goals. And, rubbing salt into my wounds was the fact that all the other scholarship holders had kicked my ass – which, because I was always doing that really unhealthy thing where I compared myself to everyone around me, made me feel extremely inadequate and very, *very* ashamed of myself.

'But Danny you were writing so much that you hardly studied!' my mum exclaimed in disbelief when I told her how I felt. 'All things considered you still did really well! How can you possibly, *possibly* be so hard on yourself?'

But that wasn't how my black-or-white, all-or-nothing mind worked. The way I saw it, if you set a goal and didn't achieve it, then it meant you failed – simple as that. That's how I felt when I got 99.6 instead of a perfect 100 for my UAI at the end of high school (Australia's SAT equivalent), and it was exactly how I felt then, too.

Fucking hell! I kept swearing to myself. *I need to work harder next semester! I need to work harder so that I can get all my writing done and still have time to study for my exams and get the marks I want. If I work harder, then I won't feel this pain ever again. If I work harder, then I'll end up getting a High Distinction average and writing a great novel and then everything will be fine. It really is that simple: I just need to work harder.*

I started my second semester of uni feeling focused and determined, and like I said, I believed that if I worked really hard then I'd achieve my goals. But, I'd never in my worst nightmares imagined that in the third week, I'd meet a girl like Chanel.

It started how it often does at that age – exhilarating, enthralling, spell-binding and magical, with nothing to suggest it would ever end in disaster. The first time we kissed was at a club in Darling Harbour, with my hands in her silky brown hair; her fingers caressing my back; and our tongues intertwined all night long – only separating so that we could beam into each other's eyes. Throughout the following week, we spent hours at uni just talking and laughing together, and then on Thursday, we went on our first official date in the city on a cloudless sunny day. We found ourselves holding hands across the table at lunch, strolling through Hyde Park with our arms around each other, sharing a big bowl of mixed gelato and feeding each other spoonfuls, and then making out beneath the trees at the Royal Botanic Gardens. In the afternoon we sat hand-in-hand on the grass and leapt into each other's souls, and I found myself telling her things I'd hardly spoken of before. I told her about how I'd always wanted to be a professional basketball player, and about how gut-wrenchingly devastated I was when I hurt my knee in Year 9 and lost my chance. I told her how that up until then I'd never bothered studying and had been ranking in the bottom 10% of the year, and that once I'd gotten injured and had no chance of playing professionally anymore, nearly everyone at my school said that I was washed up and would amount to nothing. I told her that they all looked down on me so much and made me feel so inadequate that I vowed to start studying really hard and kick all their asses in Year 12. I told her that even though high school was ancient history, that the whole experience had ignited this lasting obsession in me to want to beat everyone in everything I did, to always want to be the best, and to always want to be the guy that everyone looked up to instead of being a loser that everyone ridiculed and laughed at. Chanel listened, she understood, she shared the tribulations she'd been through. It all just happened so naturally, with an intimacy and tenderness deeper than any I'd ever known.

When night had blanketed the sky, I walked her to her platform at Central Station. We looked into each other's eyes, and not for the first time, I marvelled at how spectacularly blue hers were, which I found all the more alluring given her olive-skinned complexion. We kissed until her train came, and as I watched her board the carriage and the vehicle grow smaller and smaller in the distance, I remember feeling the tug of love at my heart, which was a dazed sort of bliss I'd never experienced before. In my ignorance, I had a good feeling about her. A really, really good feeling indeed.

Like I said, it had all started off so sublimely. I thought I'd found the woman of my dreams, and within a few weeks, my mind had done that somersault it often does the first time you fall in love, and I'd convinced myself that we'd get married one day and live happily ever after. But then a sickening notion infected my mind, and began to fill me with an anxious dread.

I think Chanel has something going on with one of my best mates.

She'd keep denying it, but I'd see the way her and Brad would look at each other. I knew they talked on the phone all the time. *And if nothing is going on,* I'd always find myself fretting, *then why does she always invite him to hang out with us? Why does she at other times blow me off to spend time with him?*

We'd fight about it all the time.

'I'm telling you Danny, we're just *friends*,' she'd always say. 'Why do you keep putting me through all this arguing? You're a dickhead for accusing me of liking him. If you really loved me, you'd believe me.'

She'd always manage to guilt me into feeling like an asshole and letting the matter drop, and I'd find myself hanging up the phone thinking I was the bad guy.

She's right, I'd tell myself. *I'm being a jerk for not trusting her. I'm implying that she's a cheater by accusing her of two-timing. How must that make her feel? ... But* still! *This just doesn't make sense! The way she's acting, something* must *be going on!*

It was such a maddening situation. Day after day it would persecute my mind. The good times – the Botanic Gardens days – became fewer and farther between, and our relationship gradually disintegrated into one big fight. Instead of being a blessing, I came to view love as a torturous curse.

*

As you well know, dear reader, you, me and everyone else in the world have one or more ways that we cope with difficulty and stress. If our coping strategies are "healthy" – for example, if we cope by exercising, meditating or by doing arts and crafts – then we're much more likely to hold up during our most challenging times and gradually make it out of them. But, if our coping strategies are "unhealthy" – for example, if we turn to alcohol, drugs or "comfort eating" – then our pain is likely to intensify, and ultimately, those unhealthy coping strategies may contribute to us falling into depression.

Suffice it to say, I was binge drinking a lot those days – 20 standard drinks a night at least two times per week. I'd always embodied the "work hard, play hard" mantra, and getting wasted like that was my favourite way to wind down after an intense week of studying and writing. To my parents – who weren't even aware of the extent of my drinking – it was a constant cause for concern. But, I was convinced I had everything under control.

'I'm just being an 18 year old,' I'd say whenever they'd reproach me. 'Plus, I work so hard during the day, so that gives me the right to cut loose at night.'

Not to mention, I'd think, *that all the fighting with Chanel is driving me nuts, and for all I know, she could be fucking my friend right now. So don't I deserve a bottle of bourbon to relax?*

Eventually, Chanel and I split up. She finally admitted she had feelings for Brad, and even though I'd obviously suspected it, I was still absolutely heartbroken. When I was alone after it happened I burst into tears, and cried long and hard into the palms of my hands. I'd genuinely believed she was the love of my life, and now that I'd lost her, I felt so overwrought, so shattered, that I couldn't fathom myself ever recovering from such a devastating blow.

'Forget about Chanel,' my friends-not-named-Brad kept telling me. 'She was making you miserable anyway. Now, it's time to get back to hanging out with us, and maybe trying to meet a new girl and have a rebound fling. You need to start trying to have fun again, mate, because we've never seen you this unhappy before.'

So instead of staying home feeling miserable, I took their advice, and pushed myself to meet up with them at bars and go out to parties. It was hard-going at first, since I was missing Chanel like crazy and I just wanted to be with her. But after a few weeks, I began to turn the corner. I started forgetting about Chanel and got back to enjoying a life of studying, writing, playing basketball, tutoring high school students and having fun with my friends. I started realising that maybe I didn't need her, that my life was actually better without all of the fighting and the drama. I even met another girl at a party and was contemplating asking her out – but then Chanel caught wind of it and hit the roof.

'I can't believe you're going to start dating someone else already!' she yelled into the phone. 'It's only been *three weeks!'*

'Are you kidding me? Chanel, *you're* the one who broke up with me because you said you liked Brad!'

'I didn't think you'd start seeing someone else so soon!'

'What did you expect me to do? Spend the rest of my life crying over you?'

'No, but – '

'Why are we even having this conversation? Shouldn't you be off fucking Brad?'

'Don't say that!'

'Why not?'

'Look – I made a mistake, OK?'

'What are you talking about?'

And then, she went on to say that she'd been really confused – that at the time we broke up she hadn't been sure what she'd wanted, but that since then she'd had a chance to figure everything out. She said that she no longer had feelings for Brad – that that was all well and truly over with and was just one big mistake. And then, she said she still had feelings for me.

Like a dog that'd been kicked in the morning but then petted at night, I was exhilarated, and had completely forgotten about the way Chanel had stomped on my heart. I was a sucker in love, and hearing her say that she still liked me was heavenly music to my ears.

'So do you want to go out again?' I asked excitedly.

'I can't,' she said.

'What? Why not?'

She said she wasn't ready to be in a relationship yet – that she needed some time to "focus on herself".

'But I will be ready soon, though, and I want you to wait for me until that time.'

I felt uneasy right away.

'You ... you want me to ... *wait* ... for you?' I asked hesitantly.

'Yes.'

'Well ... I mean ... how long for?'

'Not very long. Just until the end of the semester.'

'Why can't we just go out now?'

'I told you – I'm not ready yet.'

'Why not?'

'I don't know. I'm just not.'

I was suspicious. What she was saying didn't seem to make sense. And, I still didn't fully trust her after the fiasco with Brad.

'Danny …' she chided, sensing my reservations. 'Why are you being so misunderstanding?'

'I'm trying to understand, but – '

'I thought you loved me. Can't you just do this one little thing for the girl you love?'

More guilt trips. More manipulation. With hindsight, I shouldn't have capitulated. I shouldn't have let myself get sucked back into a situation that I didn't feel comfortable in. But, I was blinded by love and wanted nothing more than to be with her.

'OK, Chanel,' I said. 'I'll wait for you.'

*

As per our "agreement", we weren't together, but we also weren't allowed to be with anybody else, and there was the clear understanding that we'd be a couple again as soon as Chanel was "ready for a relationship".

I hated it.

Breaking up with her was devastating, but at least I had closure and could begin to heal by moving on. Under this new set of circumstances though, I got the worst of both worlds. I was stuck in no man's land. I was miserable.

'I can't stand this, Chanel,' I'd continuously tell her. 'There's just too much uncertainty ... too much that can go wrong. I mean, what if you decide that you don't want to commit to me? What if you decide you'd rather be with Brad?'

'Danny how many times do I have to tell you? There's nothing going on between me and Brad – we're just *friends!* I want to be with *you*, OK? I just need you to wait for me until I'm ready.'

'I hate this waiting, Chanel. You know I hate it ...'

'Yeah, I know. But if you love me, you'll do it.'

And so I did, and so throughout October, I grew more and more anxious, more and more distraught – and all that worry and despair poisoned the rest of my life. It made it so difficult to study and write, which meant that just like the previous semester, I fell behind in class all over again, and I didn't get anywhere near as much of my novel written as I'd wanted to.

And, just like the previous semester, I was livid with myself for it.

Do you want all the other scholarship holders to kick your ass again? I'd berate myself. *Do you want to feel inadequate again? Do you want to feel like a hopeless, pathetic, worthless failure? No? Then fucking pull yourself together and knuckle down and focus!*

But no matter how hard I tried I just couldn't do it. Chanel was tearing me apart – so much so that at times, I thought I should just tell her I wanted out and end things myself.

If I was single, I rationalised, *then I'd be able to focus and achieve my goals, and then I wouldn't feel so disappointed and frustrated and angry with myself all the time.*

But I couldn't leave her. For whatever reason, I thought she was "the one". At times I really, genuinely believed she was the one. I clung to the hope that we were just going through a rough patch, and that soon we'd get through it and then all my struggle would've been worth it.

After all, she knows how much I care about her, I convinced myself. *She'd never do anything to hurt me. We're going to get married one day and spend the rest of our lives together.*

But after the end-of-year exams were finished, Chanel told me that she'd changed her mind – that she liked being single and that she no longer had any intention to resume dating me again. I begged her to tell me why, I begged her to tell me what had changed, but she just kept reiterating that she wanted to remain unattached.

'Is this because of Brad?' I finally asked in dismay.

'No! For the last time, Brad and I are just *friends*! It's not because of him or any other guy! I just don't want to be in a relationship right now.'

Once again, I was completely and utterly crushed. That night, I went to a rat-hole of a club and got piss-blind drunk – just having one drink after another after another after another, desperately trying to drown out the anguish, to suppress the agonising grief that was all I could feel. Eventually I took a cab to my best friend Casey's house, where he consoled me for the rest of the night.

'It j-just hurts so m-much, mate,' I stuttered, holding back tears. 'I waited weeks for her, you know? And now all of a sudden … all of a sudden she just says it's over …'

'I'm really sorry, bro,' he said.

'I love her s-so much, man. All I want is just to be with her …'

'I know you do mate, I know you do,' he said, clapping me on the back.

I wiped my eyes, and with his arm around me, he continued consoling me into the early hours of the morning.

'At least you can move on now, though,' he said, once I'd finally calmed down a bit. 'You can start to forget about her and get on with your life.'

I sighed deeply.

'Yeah …'

'This is it, man,' he continued. 'No more Chanel. Just cut off all contact from her – just leave her in the past. It's all about the future now, OK? It's all about the future now.'

*

I was only studying three subjects that semester – one fewer than usual so that I could have more time to write. Given that I was doing less than a full course load, I didn't think there was any excuse for not getting a High Distinction average. So, when I only got 82% instead of my desired 85%, I was furious with myself.

What the fuck is wrong with me? I yelled in my head. *I was only doing three fucking subjects, and I* still *couldn't achieve my goal! That's fucking hopeless! That's fucking pathetic! And I can't even say that the reason I messed up was because I was writing so much, because I didn't get that much of my book written at all. It still isn't even finished yet! The reason I screwed up was because I spent the whole fucking semester fighting with and fretting over and worrying about Chanel. I was so fucking lovesick that I let her get in the way of achieving my goals. That's fucking disgraceful. That's fucking embarrassing. I should be ashamed of myself that's so fucking pitiful. I fucked up. I failed. Again! Just like I have in everything I've tried to do this year.*

*

The following week, a mutual friend of Chanel and I organised a party at a club, and regrettably, we both ended up going. As usual, I got really drunk, and then at some point in the night, I found myself talking to a girl I knew from high school. After a few more drinks, we started openly flirting with each other – until Chanel got upset and another fight ensued.

'I can't believe you've moved on already! It's only been a week!'

'Look, I haven't exactly moved on,' I said honestly. 'I still love you, OK, and I still want to be with you. But, you don't feel the same way, so it's over, and given that it is, you have no right to get pissed off with me for talking to other chicks.'

'I'm not pissed off. I just got so jealous seeing you flirt with another girl.'

'Why did you get jealous?'

'Because I still have feelings for you.'

'Then why aren't we dating then?'

'I told you! I don't want to date anyone right now.'

'Even though you have feelings for me?'

'Yes.'

I sighed.

'Does this have anything to do with Brad?'

'Shut the fuck up about Brad!' she screamed. 'How many times do I have to tell you it's got nothing to do with him?'

For a while, no-one spoke. Immeasurable frustration hung in the air as we both brooded in silence.

'So we like each other, but we're not going to date,' I eventually summed up. 'So where does that leave us?'

She shrugged.

'I don't know.'

So there I found myself again, trapped between a rock and a hard place – that insufferable no man's land I'd so hated before where we weren't together, but I wasn't free of her and moving on either.

'I'm so confused,' Chanel would always say. 'I know I have feelings for you, but I just don't want to be in a relationship right now. This is crazy, Danny. I have no idea what to do. Nothing makes sense to me anymore …'

I should've called it quits, but at the time, I had it in my mind that the reason she didn't want to be with me was because she was scared – of commitment, of intimacy, of who knows what. So, I tried to be patient with her – even though the pain of not being with her, and the fear that I could end up heartbroken all over again was so tormenting, so excruciating that as the month wore on, I gradually lost my ability to function. I could hardly write. I could barely eat. I'd lie up night after night unable to fall asleep, stressing and fretting that maybe the real reason Chanel wasn't committing to me was because she still had feelings for Brad – and that for all I knew, at that very moment she may've been fucking him.

By Christmas, however, I couldn't take it anymore. I'd devolved into an exhausted, anxious, miserable shell of myself, and I knew that something had to give. That something had to change.

'I can't keep going like this, Chanel,' I finally told her. 'It's just too much uncertainty, too much worrying, too much pain. I need to know where I stand with you – once and for all this time.'

I sighed.

'So, I'm going to give you until New Year's Eve to work out what you want. If you decide you want to be with me, then that's great. But if you don't, then I'm done with you for good. I'm moving on. For real, this time.'

New Year's Eve, 2007

From the moment I woke up I was stricken with nerves, so I went to a friend's place and tried to cope with my distress the only way I knew how: by getting drunk. By five o'clock I'd had half a dozen beers and a bottle of bourbon, and I was able to escape my heartache for two hours by passing out on the couch. But when I woke up it was time to go to the party where I'd be meeting Chanel, and once again I was consumed with worry and fear.

After a short taxi ride, my mates and I arrived and joined the other guests on the balcony. We sat in a circle and talked for a while, drinking beers and passing joints as my anxiety heightened.

Chanel's going to be here any minute! my mind kept racing. *I'm only moments away from knowing whether she'll be my girlfriend or an ex I'll never speak to again. Soon, I'm going to be either deliriously happy or disastrously heartbroken ...*

A touch after eight-thirty, she finally arrived looking beautiful as ever, wearing a white strapless dress and red high heels. With my whole body shaking, I walked up to her and gave her a peck on the cheek, and said hello to the friends she'd come with. A couple of my mates then went to greet her, and one of them ended up getting in an involved conversation with her just out of earshot. As soon as she left him to go to the bathroom, he came right up to me.

'You're in, buddy,' he grinned. 'Tonight's going to go great for you!'

Instantly filled with nervous excitement, I mixed up another big bottle of bourbon and cola and finally got talking to her myself. She was shooting me flirtatious looks, teasing me playfully, and rubbing my arm whenever she spoke. The vibe was good. The signs were all there. At some point we got drawn into a drunken group hug, and as we pulled away, our eyes locked. Our heads moved closer together. And then for the first time in almost two months, we kissed.

It was slow. Ardent. Breathtaking. Her arms were wrapped around me, clutching me tightly as I zestfully ran my fingers through her thin brown hair. Our hearts were pounding quickly, and our bodies were one as we rediscovered each other's lips, wrestled each other's tongues, leapt into each other's mouths. When we finally pulled away, we gazed into each other's eyes with giddy smiles on our faces, and in that moment, I remember thinking that everything was right with the world. I remember thinking that it had all been worth it: all of the fighting, all of the angst, all of the despair – even the disruption to my degree and my novel – because everything had turned out so wonderfully in the end. After all, it was New Year's Eve and I was on a balcony overlooking stunning Sydney Harbour, kissing the girl who I was now convinced I'd be spending the rest of my life with. I felt spectacular! On top of the world!

But then, Brad started yelling at Chanel.

'If you're just going to hook up with Danny all night, then I'm going to leave!'

He stormed away. Chanel went after him.

'Just hold on a second, OK?' she said over her shoulder to me.

I could see them at the foot of the steps that led to the street. They were discussing something with each other, and I was making small-talk with someone else – just passing the time until Chanel and I could get back to making out on the balcony. I was fantasising about kissing her on the dot of midnight, seeing in the new year with her wrapped in my arms, and then taking her back to my place so we could celebrate it properly. I thought it was going to be one of those magical nights that we'd never forget, one of those treasured memories we'd one day share with our children: the night when Mummy and Daddy got back together again …

Those were the thoughts that were dancing through my mind when I saw her kiss Brad.

My jaw dropped. I stared at them bewildered. Aghast. But on some level, I always knew.

Chanel saw me gaping at them, and quickly jumped up and pulled me into a spare room. Of course I was furious. I accused her of lying to me the entire time.

'No! No!' she protested. 'That was just a drunken mistake! Brad means nothing to me! *You're* the one I want!'

She started kissing me and then Brad got pissed off, so he pulled her away to talk to her. I sat stewing by myself as all the anguish and the stress and the misery of the last five months came roaring right back before my best friend Casey put the nail in the coffin:

'I'm sorry bro, but I just overheard her telling Brad the same thing that she just told you – that kissing *you* was a mistake, that *you* mean nothing to her, and that *he's* the one she's always wanted.'

The rest of the night was a disaster. As the fireworks brought in 2008, the three of us yelled and screamed at each other in the middle of the street, while a bunch of our friends watched on around us.

'You always said that Danny was just your *friend!*' Brad yelled at her. 'You always said that he was obsessed with you but that you never liked him! You always said that no matter how many times you told him it was over he never got the message!'

'What the fuck!' I yelled. 'Chanel, the whole time you were telling *me* –'

'No! No!' she screamed. 'Both of you – just settle down! Brad, let me talk to you for a moment. Danny, don't go anywhere – I want to talk to you afterwards.'

By then it was obvious she'd been leading a double life, particularly since she kept trying to separate Brad and me to prevent us from comparing stories. On one such occasion, I remembered that I had her six day old, $1,200 iPhone that had been imported from overseas for Christmas. Chanel had clearly been lying through her teeth, so I decided to read through the messages she'd been sending Brad to try and get closer to the bottom of what'd been going on. Within a minute, I found a text she'd sent him three days earlier.

'You're my soulmate,' it read.

I was more enraged than I'd ever been in my life

'I feel like smashing this fucking phone,' I told Casey.

'Do it,' he said.

'Do it,' the rest of my mates said.

I'd been drinking for the past 12 hours – nearly half a case of beer, the first bottle of bourbon, and a good portion of the second bottle of bourbon too – not to mention that I'd also smoked a joint.

So, I smashed it to pieces.

Eventually, Chanel and Brad went their separate ways, and that was the end of it. I stayed at the party, furious and shattered beyond belief. My mates did their best to comfort me, but there really wasn't a whole lot they could do. Eventually, I decided to go home, and as I waited for a taxi on the side of the street, I found myself feeling so utterly overwhelmed, so horrifically distraught that I collapsed by the gutter. I started coughing up bile, began trembling uncontrollably, and in that moment, I couldn't envision myself ever recovering from such a ghastly nightmare.

I was racked with grief. There was just so much pain bottled up inside me. I was irate at the fact that I was always being lied to, and by the way that Chanel had so ruthlessly betrayed me. I was embarrassed as hell that she'd played me in front of everyone. And above all else, I was heartbroken that I was all alone after I thought I'd found "the one". I'd never felt so crushed before. Never been so devastated. It was the worst time of my life.

But on the other hand, I knew I needed to move on. I felt I was at a crossroads – I could either collapse and fall apart or pull myself together and get on with my life – and I knew I needed to do the latter.

I can't change what happened in the past, I told myself, *but I can control what I do from this point forward. And, what I need to do now is forget about everything that happened last year and channel all my energy into achieving my goals. I need to work my ass off to get* Chrysalis *finished, and once uni starts, I need to study really hard so that I can get a High Distinction average. Last New Year's Eve was a mess, but if I work hard this year, then I can spend the next one celebrating getting really good marks and publishing my novel. That's the right way to respond to this – by achieving my goals. If I achieve my goals, then I'll be happy again – just like I was when I first started uni.*

Over the next few weeks, there was still a lot of anger festering inside me, but I did my best to forget about Chanel and try to move forwards. It was hard to write with a clear head, but I managed to edit *Chrysalis* to the point where I thought it was ready to be published, before deciding to get it professionally critiqued just to make sure. I caught a break and was lucky enough to be put in touch with Nick Bleszynski – an author who'd written three bestsellers and mentored two writers who ended up signing major publishing deals.

Once he's read my manuscript, I'll make the changes he suggests and then submit it for publication, I thought.

I figured that after that I'd then be able to switch my attention to my degree, and I was confident that without my novel to worry about, that I'd be able to study as much as I needed to in order to get a High Distinction average.

*

In February, I also decided to spend the money I'd saved tutoring to visit South America at the end of the year, so that I could volunteer at an underprivileged school in Cusco, Peru. I'd found out about the opportunity from a friend, but it was Mr Williams' words at the scholarship dinner the previous year that had made me want to do it:

'You've been blessed with so much,' he'd told me. 'You've been brought up in a wonderful neighbourhood; you're surrounded by a loving, supportive family; and you've got the opportunity and the ability to do anything you want to in life. I hope you always use your blessings for good. I hope you always do charity work, and I hope you always try to help people. Remember, Danny: to whom much is given, much is expected.'

He's right, I thought. *Even though I've been going through a tough time lately, I'm still a very lucky person. I've been blessed with so much like Mr Williams said, and it's my responsibility to start giving back, and lend a helping hand to those less fortunate than myself.*

I did *not* rape her.

But that's the rumour I started hearing when I got back to uni.

'To justify her intimacy with you to Brad, Chanel said that you'd force yourself on her. She said that she wouldn't want you to but that you wouldn't take no for an answer.'

I couldn't believe it. I seriously couldn't believe it. I cherished that girl every day we were together. I treated her like a queen. I would've turned the world upside down to make her happy. So to have her accuse me of something as vile and despicable as rape made me sick to my stomach. It made me so fucking angry.

It made me so fucking angry that I wanted to kill her.

This is not hyperbole – I literally wanted to kill her.

I never, ever would've actually done so. I strongly believe the best revenge in these cases is simply living well. I knew that the right way of responding to everything she'd put me through was to channel my fury into achieving my goals and then go on to live a happy life. I did know that, and that's what I was focused on doing. But after I heard those allegations ... I'd be lying to you if I said I never got the urge to pick up a baseball bat and smash in her face. I was that enraged.

I mean, lying to me throughout our whole relationship was bad enough.

Two-timing with one of my best friends was even worse.

But spreading rumours that I'd *raped* her?

I don't even know what you call betrayal that extreme, and to this day, it's the most heart-wrenching, scarring thing anyone has ever done to me.

Week after week, my heartbreak, my fury, and my complete and utter disgust at the rape rumours continued to eat away at me, and what made it even worse was the impact it was having on my ability to achieve my goals. While I'd be in class I'd often find myself too distraught to focus, just like I would be when I'd be studying at home or even sitting an exam. Consequently, I didn't get High Distinctions, and of course the other scholarship holders did, and as usual, that made me feel like a hopeless, pathetic, inadequate failure.

And then, I received Nick's editorial report for *Chrysalis,* which said that while the story wasn't without potential, *a lot* of improvements needed to be made since the writing style was "terrible"; there were too many "clichéd similes, unnecessary big words, awkwardly-worded sentences and melodramatic scenes"; the historical aspects of the book were "very poorly researched"; the love story between the two main characters was "not believable"; the motifs were "amateurish"; the poetry I'd inserted here and there was "awful"; my use of punctuation was "neither proper nor effective"; and the ending was "contrived".

And of course, being the achievement-orientated person I was, that made me hate myself even more.

Adolescents need to be educated about depression.

In my humble opinion, they need to be educated about depression in school, and they also need to be educated about depression at home – in the same way they're educated about safe sex and drink driving.

Why? Because if they find themselves experiencing the symptoms, they can then realise that they're suffering from an illness, and then go and get treatment.

But if they don't know what depression is, then they won't seek help, and will thus prolong their suffering.

They might self-medicate with drugs and alcohol and develop an addiction.

They might self-harm by ripping out their hair, cutting themselves with razors, or lighting parts of their body on fire.

And worst of all, they might kill themselves.

Some parents think of depression as something that's "too dark" for their teenager to be exposed to. If you're one of those people, then let me give you some stats:

At the time of writing, in the US, the UK and Australia, as many as 20% of teens will experience depression before they reach adulthood.

Measuring rates of self-harm has proved difficult for a variety of reasons, but there have been studies that estimate that 6-7% of 15-24 year olds intentionally hurt themselves, and other studies that suggest the figures are as high as 12-20%.

For youths aged 15-24, suicide is the third leading cause of death in America.

For the same age group, it is the second leading cause of death in the UK.

And for the same cohort in Australia, it is *the* leading cause.

Depression is persecuting youths all over the globe. It's a worldwide epidemic that's everywhere you turn – even if you don't know it, even if some of the sufferers themselves don't know it. Regardless of age, gender, sexuality, religion, colour or creed, teens are at risk for a myriad of reasons – so isn't it best that they're educated to spot the warning signs if they do fall victim?

The reason I bring all of this up is because when I was 19, I couldn't have known any less about depression. I knew what I was feeling – in the sense that I knew I was emotionally struggling – but I had no idea I was starting to develop an illness. If I did I would've gotten the help I needed, and this story would probably end right here.

But alas, it continues ...

Around that time – in the aftermath of the rape rumours, Nick's extremely disappointing book review, and the fact that I only got a 76% average in my exams that semester – I found myself having more stress, anxiety and misery to deal with than ever – and as a result, I was drinking more than ever to cope: every two nights with my friends, 25 standard drinks until I passed out.

The signs that I had a drinking problem had been there for a while, but at that point, they were getting harder and harder to ignore. My friends being worried about me was one. Craving alcohol in the middle of the day was another. Getting beaten up by a stranger outside the casino and being too wasted to understand what his problem was or to even feel the assault was the nail in the coffin.

After I finally admitted I had a problem to myself, I did the most sensible thing I'd done all year, and admitted that I had a problem to my parents. Like I said, they had no idea to what extent I'd been drinking, and when they found out, they were horrified. But regardless, they were extremely supportive as always.

'We're not here to pass judgment on you, Danny. We're your parents, and we love you, and we just want to do whatever it takes to help you get better.'

After a long talk, I agreed to see a psychologist who specialised in treating addictions – who in our two sessions together, taught me how to deal with the cravings I started to experience after 96 hours sober.

'What do cravings feel like?' people sometimes ask me.

It's pretty hard to describe, but I think the best I can do is say that craving alcohol is like being really, really, *really* hungry, and fighting it's like not eating. It's wholly consuming. There's nothing else you can think about, and nothing else you can do until it has mercy on you and passes. I remember some very, very rough nights spent sitting hunched on the edge of my bed, panting, sweating, shaking, ripping strands of hair out of my head as my whole body screamed *give me booze! Give me booze! GIVE ME BOOZE!*

'No ... no ...' I'd whisper out loud. 'Just hold off drinking for another hour ... hold off drinking for another hour ...' It's what I'd told myself an hour beforehand, and it's what I'd had to keep telling myself to get through those nights. It was a technique my psychologist had taught me – based on the premise of breaking down seemingly insurmountable tasks – like not drinking all night – into one smaller, more surmountable task at a time.

'Just hold off drinking for the next hour ...' I'd keep murmuring. 'It's only an hour ... it's only an hour ... you did it last hour so you can do it this hour too. Just stay strong ... keep fighting ... don't give in. No matter how much you want to you cannot give in ...'

By the end of the mid-semester break and my fourth week without alcohol, I felt infinitely better. My cravings had abated, my anger at Chanel had finally begun to evaporate, and I'd been able to work productively on the next draft of *Chrysalis*. For the first time in months, my mind felt relatively clear, and I felt ready and determined to throw myself into getting a High Distinction average and having my novel published by the end of the year.

Then life will be perfect again, I remember thinking. *Then I'm going to feel happy again – just like I did when I first started uni.*

If I'd learned about depression and mental health in school or anywhere else, then I would've known that it's extremely dangerous to pin your happiness, self-confidence or your value as a person to the achievement of a goal, or to any other form of external validation. It's far more emotionally sound to love-, value- and respect yourself "from the inside out" – and later on in this book, I'll elaborate on what that means and how to do it. Suffice it to say though, in 2008, I didn't know about any of that stuff, and as a result, I was in far more trouble than I ever could've realised.

PART II:

IT'S REALLY HARD TO GET BETTER IF YOU DON'T GET HELP

In my novel *I Will Not Kill Myself, Olivia,* Jimmy and his girlfriend always thought they'd get married and spend the rest of their lives together … that is, until college, when Jimmy starts suffering from depression. From that point on in the story, I start exploring what happens to them when their relationship becomes a threesome: i.e. Jimmy, Olivia, and the serious mental illness.

What sort of chaos can it lead to?

How does it change their relationship? Does it bring both of them closer together or does it rip them apart?

Is Olivia's love and support enough to help Jimmy through it, or does he still need to receive professional treatment?

And, even if Jimmy does manage to recover, will his relationship with Olivia ever be the same?

I never had a girlfriend throughout my war with depression like Jimmy did, but I did have a close friend called Sylvia, who if truth be told, was the inspiration for Olivia herself. The two situations were hardly the same – Jimmy and Olivia were ardent lovers who wanted to spend forever together, whereas Sylvia and I were friends living on opposite sides of the world. Nevertheless, we often used to reach out to each other for advice and support, and some of the relationship-related questions I explore in my novel were based on real life events that happened between Sylvia and myself.

And so, she enters this story with a Facebook message:

> *Hey Sylvia,*
>
> *I thought I was better. I honestly thought I'd beaten it. But somehow, I feel completely miserable again. It's not about*

Chanel so much – I think I'm finally getting over all of that – but even still, I just haven't been able to find a balance between studying and writing. I mean for fuck's sake – I've only been back at uni six weeks, and I'm already behind in all of my subjects, and I haven't written that much of my novel either. I feel like such a loser – since I've been at uni a year-and-a-half now and I'm STILL having these issues! I feel like such an idiot. Every semester I've had at uni has been a failure, and I'm well on my way to failing this one too.

My only solution is to work harder. I think if I could study and write for a total of 60 hours a week, then I should be able to achieve my goals. I think working 60 hours a week would allow me to get a lot of studying and writing done, and still give me enough time to tutor high school kids, coach basketball, play basketball, go to the gym, and go out with my friends. Then again, maybe 60 hours a week isn't enough either. Maybe I need to be pushing myself harder. Maybe I should be working 70 hours a week. Maybe 80. Maybe more. I mean, I'm going to feel miserable until my novel's published and I've achieved a High Distinction average, right? So maybe I shouldn't be doing anything else apart from studying and writing. Fucking hell ... I don't know. I just feel so overwhelmed. Everything seems so hopeless. I've lost so much confidence. So much self-belief. I never thought I'd say this, but I don't know if I can achieve my goals anymore.

I hope you can say something to help, Sylvia. I'm really struggling at the moment and could use your support.

Love,

Danny.

She replied a few days later:

Hey Danny,

I'm so sorry to hear that you're going through such a hard time again. I know it must be tough being so unhappy and feeling like you can't achieve your goals, but whatever you do, just keep hanging in there. You've faced some really hard challenges before and you've always overcome them, and I know you're going to do the same here too. Remember back in high school, when you never used to study and all you cared about was basketball? You were so devastated when you injured your knee and had no chance of playing professionally anymore – and because you were in the bottom 10% of the year everyone said you were dumb and would amount to nothing – but you turned your life around, and ended up graduating in the top 0.4% of the state. I've always found your ability to overcome setbacks really inspiring, and I know you're going to overcome this one, too. You're one of the strongest people I know, Danny. Honestly – I've never met anyone with the kind of will power and determination you have! So please remember that, and know that it will let you achieve what you want. It always has.

But, at the same time, it might be a good idea to try and not always be so hard on yourself. Seriously, Danny – you always put so much pressure on yourself to achieve such difficult goals, and that's really what seems to be making you so unhappy right now. I mean, if you get an average of 75 or 80% instead of 85%, is it really the end of the world? Those marks are still really good by almost anyone's standards! And what about your novel? Does it really matter if you finish it and get it published this year or the next? Either way you'll have written and published a book, right? That's incredible! How many other 19 year olds can say that?

But aside from that, Danny, just keep at it. Keep believing in yourself, keep having faith in God, and know that I believe in you too.

You can do this – I know you can.
Love always,
Sylvia.

Ever since we'd become close friends, Sylvia had had a way of filling me with hope. Having her say that she believed in me meant everything, because I wasn't someone who was used to being believed in. My family were great and had faith in me no matter what, but aside from them, I was always being doubted. Like Sylvia alluded to, when I started trying hard in school after I'd hurt my knee, everyone laughed at me and said I'd fail – just like they did after I'd done really well in school and told them I was going to write a novel.

'You've got to be joking!' they all cackled. 'You're only good at "maths" subjects. English was your worst by far. You can't write. You struggled with *essays,* for crying out loud! So how do you, of all people, think you can possibly get a novel published?'

I'm going to do it because I have the right attitude to succeed, I'd think. *I have a tireless work ethic and relentless determination, and I never, ever, ever give up. That's how I managed to overcome my knee injury and get a scholarship to law school, and it's also how I'm going to get my novel published. With the attitude I have, anything is possible, and even though I may struggle and fall, I'll get up every time and get what I'm going for in the end.*

But aside from my family, Sylvia was the only one who saw that, which is why I cherished her belief in me so much. In fact, I treasured it even more than my family's faith in me – for the same reason that it means more to a teenage girl when the football captain says she's beautiful than when she hears it from her father. Having Sylvia say that she had confidence in me and that I had what it took to achieve my goals always gave me hope. It gave me strength. It inspired me. And, when I felt hopeful, strong and inspired, I stopped feeling miserable.

I didn't agree with what Sylvia said at the end of her message, though – that it didn't really matter if I only got 80% instead of 85%, or if *Chrysalis* got published later than I hoped.

I need to be at the top of the cohort! I always pressured myself. *I need to be the best! And 80% is not the best. A few of the other scholarship holders get High Distinction averages, so that means that I have to get a High Distinction average, too. Anything less is unacceptable. Anything less is a failure. And, I also need to finish* Chrysalis *this year and get it published as soon as possible, because as much as I enjoy working on it, it's a huge disruption to my degree, and getting a High Distinction average would be a whole lot easier if I wasn't writing a book at the same time.*

So I was convinced that Sylvia wasn't right on that front. Instead, I thought the solution was to just work harder.

If I can work for a total of 60 hours a week, I reasoned, *then I should be able to achieve my goals and then everything will be fine.*

October, 2008

But unfortunately, even working 60 hours a week was nowhere near enough to be able to keep up with uni and progress with my novel at a meaningful pace – and as a result, I continued to spiral further downwards. To chart my descent, I've included some diary entries that capture my anguish at the time – an anguish that you're likely to find eerily familiar.

October 3, 2008

Life is such a fight, such an all-out slog. All I do is work – work, work, work – so much so that all the enjoyment has been drained from my life. But despite how hard I push myself, I still can't achieve my goals ... which makes me feel like a failure, and that makes me work even harder in response, and working even harder makes me feel even more miserable, and when I still can't achieve my goals I feel like even more of a failure, and the worst part of this ghastly nightmare is that I can't see anything ever changing. I can't envision myself ever getting out of it. And when I feel that hopeless, I start craving booze. All I want to do is lock myself in my room with a litre bottle of bourbon and drink and drink and drink until I eventually pass out. And when I feel that in need of the bottle, I can't study properly, I can't write properly, and then I start to hate myself for not working effectively, and then to drown out the self-loathing I want to drink even more, and then I'm even more unable to function, and then it's even harder to achieve my goals, and so the cycle goes. So what the fuck am I supposed to do? What the fuck am I supposed to do? WHAT THE FUCK AM I SUPPOSED TO DO?

October 9, 2008

I'm fucking hopeless. I'm fucking pathetic. I'm such a lazy fucking piece of shit. Who the fuck can't work 60 hours a week to achieve their goals? It doesn't matter how exhausted I am. It doesn't matter how dreadful I feel. Only working 54 hours this week is a fucking disgrace. It's fucking pathetic. I'm such a fucking slacker. I should be ashamed of myself I'm so fucking lazy.

October 14, 2008

Sylvia,

I'm cracking, I'm breaking at the seams – because no matter how hard I work I keep on failing, and every day, I feel more and more miserable. I'll keep on fighting to get out of this mess – because as you know I am not a quitter – but right now, all my struggle seems to be in vain. I just can't see how I'm ever going to achieve my goals, and so I can't see how I'm ever going to be happy. And somehow even after all these months, there are days when I still feel so full of anger towards Chanel. I just still can't believe she told people I raped her! How the fuck could she actually tell people I raped her?!

Put all this together and I'm desperate to drink. The cravings are insufferable. I try to fight them off but they won't go away. They just keep growing, more and more intense. So I thought I'd Facebook you. It was literally either that or getting smashed.

Please say something, anything to help.

Love,

Danny.

October 17, 2008

For the third time this week, I spent the night on the edge of my bed dripping with sweat, gripping my hair, gasping through gritted teeth in desperation for the bottle. I just wanted to forget everything, just wanted to escape. But, because I knew it wasn't right, instead of drinking I printed off Sylvia's response from Facebook, held it tightly in my hands, and read it over and over and over again.

You're so strong, Danny, *she'd written.* You're going to overcome this – just like you've overcome every other difficulty you've faced. Everything is going to turn out well, and all your dreams are going to come true. I know it, Danny. I just know it.

They're the only words that kept me sober.

October 21, 2008

What the fuck is wrong with me? I tell myself I'm a hard worker, I tell myself I have the discipline to achieve my goals, but then this week I only manage to work 53 hours? There are no excuses – that's fucking atrocious. That's a fucking disgrace. I'm such a fucking slacker. Such a worthless fucking piece of shit.

This cannot happen anymore. This cannot happen ever-fucking-again! If it ever does, then I deserve to be punished! So from now on, any time I don't work 60 hours a week, I'm going to cut myself with a steak knife. Starting just above the wrist, I'm going to sink the blade into my forearm and then rip it through my flesh. Maybe then I won't be so lazy. Maybe then I won't fucking fail so much.

October 24, 2008

I'm fucking wasted. It just happened – I snapped and drank a bottle of bourbon alone in my room. Even Sylvia's message couldn't save me. All the anxiousness, the misery, the pressure, how overwhelmed I felt ... it became unbearable. I was desperate for an escape and I didn't know how else to get it.

Late October, 2008

The thing about depression is that if you don't seek help, then not only is it almost impossible to recover, but you'll also tend to continue spiralling further and further downwards – which is why a few days after I broke my three month sober stretch, I had my first fantasy about death. It was four o'clock in the morning, and I was cramming for a statistics exam I was way behind on.

'You're going to fail, you're going to fail,' whispered a voice in my head.

'You're going to fail, you're going to fail.'

I tried to block it out, I tried to forget about it, but no matter what I did it was always there heckling me, taunting me.

'You're so far behind … you'll never catch up … you're going to fail … again … just like you always do …'

It fed my fear, heightened it, made me want to scream.

'You're going to fail, you're going to fail.'

I need an escape, I thought. *I need a break.*

'You're going to fail, you're going to fail.'

Need booze. Fucking gagging for it.

'You're going to fail, you're going to fail.'

Shut up! Shut the fuck up!

'You're going to fail! You're going to fail!'

I want to die! I want to die! I hate my life so much that I just want to die!

At that moment, the "low battery" notification flashed across the screen of my laptop:

Only 10% remaining. Connect to a power source immediately.

I retrieved the charger from my bag, and as I was about to insert it into the power point, I remember hoping that something would go wrong – that there'd be some sort of malfunction – so that when I plugged in the chord I'd be electrocuted to death. And, when I was still alive afterwards, I remember feeling dejected. I remember feeling disappointed that I was still breathing in a world I no longer wanted to be a part of.

The good news is that I was able to make it through my exams without cutting myself. But, the bad news is that my average that semester was only 74%, and after it was over, I felt more like a failure than ever – in addition to feeling exhausted, fed-up, frustrated, and completely and utterly miserable.

Despite feeling the worst I'd ever felt in my life, though, I didn't reach out for help – since at the time, I was still convinced that I was just going through a rough patch, and that if I could just achieve my goals, I would then stop hating myself. Instead, after talking things over with my parents, I decided to ease my workload the following year – by only taking two subjects instead of my usual eight subject course load (which the university allowed). The way I saw it, having effectively a year off uni would give me time to finish my novel and get it published, after which, I could then return to my degree feeling refreshed and committed, and without my novel to work on, actually be able to study hard and get a High Distinction average.

It was a good idea, but when it comes to depression, usually changing your circumstances is not enough to beat it. What I needed even more so – just like almost everyone fighting this excruciating condition – was therapy.

Why, you may ask?

Because through therapy, I could've learned how to re-wire the way I thought, and therefore learned how to handle life's difficulties in a more psychologically-sound way that wouldn't have caused me to feel depressed. But like I said, at that time I didn't reach out for help, and until the day I did, my broken mind never healed.

December, 2008

Now that my exams were finished and I didn't have to study, I felt better, but I was still far from happy. The last time I was happy – which was when I started university – felt like a lifetime ago, and when I pictured the smiling, confident, exuberant young man I'd been at the scholarship dinner, I couldn't recognise him. As is the case for most people who struggle with depression, my former cheerful self seemed like a ghost, and it was almost unfathomable to think that that person had been me.

A vivid memory I have of that time is being on my flight to South America, where I was going to do my volunteer program in Peru and some backpacking around the neighbouring countries. Before I left, everyone said that I'd have the time of my life – but when I tried to picture myself having fun, I couldn't see it. In my dismal state, the idea of pleasure seemed too foreign. Too farfetched. And in those silent, pensive hours, when the lights were switched off and all the passengers were asleep except for me, my thoughts kept returning to the same lone question:

Will I ever be happy, again?

And also to the same answer:

I don't know.

I really, genuinely, truthfully don't know.

Santiago, Chile – late December, 2008

I arrived in Chile's capital city feeling awful and desperate to have fun, so I spent most of my time there getting wasted with other backpackers. Given my history with alcoholism, I knew I shouldn't have been drinking – but I didn't care. Amidst Santiago's raging party scene, I was finally enjoying myself and that's all that mattered to me.

'Hey Danny, do you want to do some coke?' a bloke at the hostel asked while we were guzzling beers and shooting pool.

'Never had it before, bro. What's it like?'

'Oh it's so good, man! It makes you feel so alive. It makes you feel on top of the world. Two snorts and you'll be flying, man!'

I just wanted to be happy. I'd been miserable all year and I just wanted to feel happy again.

'Yeah, let's do it, dude.'

So along with a bunch of other people, we went to a club and got blazed. We stayed there all night long – dancing, drinking, snorting more cocaine and having the time of our lives just like I was promised, and, even though I knew I shouldn't have been doing it, I was just so glad to be enjoying myself again that I couldn't have cared less.

Cusco, Peru – January, 2009

Despite going through some of the toughest times of my life during my first two years at university, ever since Mr Williams had emphasised how fortunate I was at the scholarship dinner, I'd been much, much more mindful of all of my blessings – in particular, having been raised in a wonderful neighbourhood; being surrounded by a loving, supportive family; and being gifted with the opportunity and the ability to do anything I wanted to in life. But, I never knew just how lucky I was until I volunteered in Cusco, Peru – a city that's best known for being the gateway to Machu Picchu, but behind all the travel agencies and the bopping backpacker bars, is a place that's rife with poverty.

I was volunteering in the surrounding mountain villages, and before I went there, I'd never been to a place where 56% of the population lived on less than US$1 a day, where 85% of children never attended high school, where the school drop-out rate was 40%, where the unemployment rate was 42%, where the underemployment rate was 74%, where the literacy rate was 18%, where the infant mortality rate was 5%, and where the average life expectancy was 41 years.

I'd never met any children who wore the same World Vision clothes to school every day.

I'd never been to a school where not a single kid was fat, nor had I ever been called fat by anyone else – which is what some of the children thought the volunteers were because we weren't bone-skinny.

I'd never had 10 year olds try to sell me cigarettes on the street at two in the morning on a school night to help support their family.

I'd never been too embarrassed to tell someone I had a swimming pool in my backyard, like I was when my host family – who lived in a flat barely larger than my living room – had asked me to describe my home to them.

I'd never lived in a place where only ice-cold water came out of the taps, meaning that I had to heat it with a kettle and use a bucket and cup to shower.

I'd never seen villages of houses that didn't have any windows and were made out of mud bricks, much less had I helped build chimneys out of bamboo for those houses so that smoke wouldn't suffocate the air when the families cooked over a fire.

I'd never been to a place where all the adults looked 20 years older than their actual age, and where people as young as 30 had dry and wrinkled skin.

I'd never met a kid who grabbed other peoples' crotches and stuck his fingers up their bums during a school yard game of dodge ball.

'Why does he do that?' one of the volunteers asked.

'Because ... he gets sexually abused at home.'

'By who?'

The volunteer manager released a painful sigh.

'By his father.'

We were all flabbergasted.

'How come ... how come no-one's reported it?'

'We have.'

'And?'

He sighed again.

'The police ... it's not like in your country. There's so much corruption ... it's not like in your country.'

'But surely something can be done about it?'

'I'm afraid not.'

Seeing this poverty, this exploitation, this corruption, this perversion; waking up every morning and staring it in the face ... it can change you. And it certainly changed me. Like I said I was aware of it before, but working in that community made me realise just how immensely privileged I really was, and when I looked into the eyes of those skinny kids wearing World Vision clothes, I knew that it was up to me as one of the extremely fortunate people in this world to step up and give them a helping hand. So, I did whatever I could there, whether that was helping to build a chicken coup or a vegetable patch in the school so that the students could have eggs and vegies as a constant source of food; pitching in to construct a new classroom; or helping to build chimneys for the houses in the villages. And as I hammered away, I knew that that wouldn't be the end for me. I knew I wouldn't just go back to Sydney and forget about that place. I knew it was the start of something big, and that in time, I was going to be making a much bigger contribution to that community than just pounding nails.

*

But after having a great day volunteering, I'd then go out and have a great night snorting cocaine and partying. I thought being high on coke was the best feeling in the world. Whenever I took it I felt like I could run forever, fly, conquer the world. I just felt so confident, vivacious and energetic. I felt the exact opposite of depressed. And, when I was dancing on top of the bar at three in the morning, fucked out of my mind and fist-pumping like hell to the music with a crowd of other backpackers, I felt so incredible that it was hard to imagine I ever was.

New Zealand – February 7, 2009

After six weeks in South America, I went to Auckland for a week-long stopover on the way home, where I dived back in to writing my novel. I'd missed it so, so much, so every morning, I'd stroll down to a coffee shop called Esquires, order myself a milkshake and a ham and cheese croissant, and then just write, write, write. Now that I was no longer so stressed out with uni, working on my novel was back to filling me with indescribable joy, and an inner peace more serene than any I'd ever known.

This is my favourite thing to do in the world, I remember thinking to myself. *Waking up, walking to a coffee shop, and spending the whole day writing my book is truly my favourite thing to do in the whole entire world ...*

It was the perfect way to end a perfect trip, and as I was flying back to Sydney, I remember feeling ecstatic that I'd be able to spend all of 2009 focusing on writing, and ecstatic about my life in general.

Gone are the days when I feel worthless! I whole-heartedly believed. *Never again will I feel so overwhelmed that I want to lock myself in my room and drink until I'm numb, never again will I feel hopelessly miserable, and never again will I hate my life so much that I wish I was dead. Those days are ancient history, and now that I'm back to being my confident, happy and exuberant self, I'm ready to jump back into life, chase my dreams, catch them, and live happily ever after.*

Sydney – February, 2009

On my first Saturday night back home, I arranged to catch up with some friends in Darling Habour. Like I'd been doing in South America, I wanted to get drunk, but since I didn't have much money left over from my trip to spend at the bars, I started downing bourbon and colas in my room an hour-and-a-half before my friend Cal was scheduled to pick me up. By the time he'd arrived, the one litre bottle of Jim Beam was mostly finished, and I was completely shitfaced.

'Sup man?' I yelled when I opened the door.

'Danny ... are you trashed already?'

'Yeah, bro! Let's go party!'

He didn't even look shocked – and why would he? He knew my track record as well as anyone, and when he saw me the previous night, I was just as wasted.

We met the other boys at Darling Harbour and decided to go to Cargo Bar. The guys got let in, but when I went to give the bouncer my ID he shook his head.

'You can't come in tonight,' he said.

'Aawww, why not man?' I slurred.

'You've had too much to drink.'

'Naahhh, bro. You've got to let me in!'

He shook his head and told me to leave. My mates tried to talk him into letting me inside but he stood his ground.

'That guy was a fucking cock!' I said loudly as we were walking away. 'Why the fuck didn't he let me inside?'

My friends shook their heads.

'Anyway fuck Cargo!' I kept ranting. 'Let's go to Bungers!'

We lined up at Bungalow8 but it was the same story there, too. I tried again and again, hoping that a different bouncer would card me and let me in – but I was refused every time. We gave up when they threatened to blacklist me from the club and call the police if I didn't leave.

'Why are all the bouncers being such fucking assholes tonight?' I yelled.

'They're not being fucking assholes,' one of my mates finally said. 'You're wasted as hell. You shouldn't even be out.'

'Naahhh, man! They're all just being fucking assholes tonight!'

Eventually, we got let in to Strike Bar down the road. I headed straight for the bar and started knocking back cocktails.

'Stop drinking! Stop drinking!' everyone was telling me.

But I couldn't stop. When some guys go out their entire night's about trying to get laid, but with me it was all about trying to get as much booze into me as possible. Once that switch got flicked I craved it like nothing else, and then, it became all I could think about.

After two or three cocktails, I was being even more loud and obnoxious than I was beforehand. My friends grew more and more pissed off with me, and at some point, they left without saying goodbye. Cal said he'd take me home, so I stumbled into his car and passed out in the front seat.

He woke me up when we reached my house. I opened the car door but instead of going inside, I staggered away in the opposite direction. He tried to guide me back but I broke free and kept lurching away, crashing around in the neighbour's garden. Eventually he gave up and went to get my mum. It was late at night. She answered the doorbell, shocked to see him.

'Cal? What's wrong?' she panicked.

He sighed.

'Hi Mrs Baker … Danny's drunk too much. Could you please help me get him inside?'

My parents were livid the next day.

'This is disgraceful!' they screamed. 'What the hell were you thinking! You know you're not supposed to be drinking! You know that if you do you're going to ruin your life!'

They were right, of course, so as they continued berating me, I nodded my head in self-disgust and agreed with everything they said. Then when they'd stopped yelling, I started berating myself.

What the fuck is wrong with me? How the fuck do I not know by now that I can't control myself when I drink? Seriously, how the fuck can I be so stupid? How the fuck can I be so blind? I'm such a fucking idiot. Such a fucking loser. Such a stupid fucking piece of shit.

I was so appalled with myself for screwing up again. I felt so worthless. I felt like such a failure. And as a result, all the distress, misery and self-hatred from the previous year had come roaring back, and was overwhelming me with more force than ever before. It included the vehement despair that always came from feeling like a failure, but this time, my anguish was also greatly exacerbated by the fact that I'd previously tricked myself into thinking I was healthy again. After all, on the way back to Sydney, I thought I'd beaten it, remember? But as it turned out, I hadn't recovered at all – and that, more so than anything else, scared the absolute shit out of me.

I mean how the hell could I feel so good, feel so certain that I'd conquered my demons, only to feel like this again seven days later? I was panicking. *It's been a whole year now – how can I still feel so miserable after all these months?*

And then came the most terrifying fears that a person with depression can possibly have:

Will I always feel this way?

Is this just the way I am?

Will I forever be condemned to a life of endless suffering?

If at the end of the day, all people want is to be happy, then is this feeling – *will I forever be condemned to a life of endless suffering?* – not the most frightening feeling we can possibly experience?

The fact that it haunts everyone in the throes of a prolonged depression – not to mention that all such people are going through hell to begin with – is what makes clinical depression such a horrific illness.

There were days when I felt myself – when I woke up feeling cheerful, when I thoroughly enjoyed being able to write all day, and when the future seemed bright and full of promise. But like my most recent drinking incident had proven, my so-called "recovery" had been a hoax, and because I hadn't yet gone to therapy and learned how to properly deal with my depression, it meant that if my day wasn't "circumstantially perfect" – i.e. that if something throughout any given day went even slightly wrong – then I'd have a cataclysmic meltdown. In this way, it was like I was walking on a tightrope, where the tiniest hit would knock me off and send me spiralling into despair – such as missing a bus, forgetting my wallet at home, writing a paragraph for my book that I'd later deem not very good, or being five minutes late to my only class at uni. Any time something small like that would go awry, the *"what the fuck is wrong with you?"*, *"you're such a fucking idiot!"*, *"you're such a fucking failure!"* self-abuse would start, and then soon after came those horrifically confronting questions: *will I always feel this way? Is this just the way I am? Will I forever be condemned to a life of endless suffering?* They'd chill me to the bone, and the only way I knew how to handle them was by drinking. But after the "Darling Harbour Night" I promised myself I'd stop, so I had no way to fight my demons, no way to balance on the tightrope – which like I said, meant that on any given day, I was only one little nudge away from disaster.

For many people with depression, to greater or lesser degrees, this is the state in which they live their lives. As I have mentioned – and as I will literally *prove* to you later on in this book – the only way you can *permanently* break free from this state; recover from depression; and then be able to confidently, calmly and stably navigate your way through life is by:

1) Learning the reasons why *you,* specifically, struggle with depression; and
2) What *you,* specifically, need to do to overcome it.

This is exactly what you'll learn overtime in therapy – or if therapy's prohibitively expensive, what you can alternatively learn by reading self-help books written by the world's most esteemed psychologists, psychiatrists and industry professionals. But, when you don't seek help like so, this is what's almost guaranteed to happen:

1) As I have said, you will continue to spiral further and further downwards, and then eventually:
2) If you don't commit suicide, you'll convince yourself that your depression is just a part of you. You'll convince yourself that no matter what you do, it will always be there, and that no matter what you do, you will never recover. And, no matter how much people like me, or any one of the other millions of people who've recovered from this illness tell you that it's possible, you will not believe us – because your depression has tricked you into believing that regardless of anything you do, it's going to haunt you forever.

By this point in my life, I was at "Stage 1", and my next downward spiral occurred when I had a writing course – *How To Develop Romantic Relationships Between Characters* – at the New South Wales Writers' Centre in Rozelle at ten o'clock one morning. I took the 7:46 a.m. bus to Queen Victoria Building in the city from the top of my street, which was meant to get me there before nine o'clock – but the peak hour traffic was worse than usual, and it didn't arrive until 9:11. At the stop opposite QVB, I checked what time the next bus left to Rozelle.

Fucking hell, I swore.

It wasn't coming until 9:25.

That's really pushing it! I started to panic, feeling myself begin to wobble on my tightrope. *That's really fucking pushing it! What if I'm late? What if I miss a part of the class that's really important? What the fuck am I going to do then?*

At 9:25 I anxiously boarded the bus, and reached Rozelle at a quarter-to-ten. When I saw a sign that read *NSW Writers' Centre,* I pressed the button to get off – but when I disembarked a few moments later and walked back to stand in front of the sign, instead of seeing clear directions to the centre, all I saw was a big grassy area and a large complex of buildings.

Oh, shit! Oh, shit! I freaked out. *Where the fuck is this place? Where the fuck is this place?*

I frantically walked through the field, studying all the buildings – but nothing indicated that any of them were the Writers' Centre. With mounting panic I circled them once, twice, three times – but I still couldn't find where the damn place was.

And then, on came the self-abuse:

What the fuck have I done? What the fuck have I done? Why the fuck didn't I look up exactly where this place is on a fucking map? Why the fuck didn't I ask for directions? Why the fuck am I so stupid? Why the fuck am I such a fucking moron?

I checked the time on my phone: three minutes to ten.

Fucking hell! I'm going to be late! I'm going to be late! What the fuck will I do if I'm late?

I let out a loud, desperate groan and then ran back to the main road. I looked around hopelessly, desperately, but I had no idea where it was. Eventually I ran down the street before I saw one perpendicular to the road I was on: Alberto Street. It meant nothing to me. I doubled back through the field and the buildings and hysterically searched for the Writers' Centre again but to no avail. I checked the time once more: 10:10.

I'm such a cunt! I screamed in my head. *How the fuck can I not get to a fucking course on time! What the fuck is wrong with me? Why the fuck am I so pathetic? Fucking hell! I'm such a cunt, I'm such a cunt, I'm such a* cunt!

I was so angry with myself that I collapsed in a heap beneath a tree and burst into tears. I just completely broke down – so overwhelming was my vehement self-loathing, my nauseous distress, my ghastly misery that all I could do was cry and cry and cry. I sat there for what felt like hours, just bawling my eyes out, and all I could think was, *my life is so fucked up, my life is so fucked up, my life is so fucked up that I wish I was dead.* As a reader, it may be hard for you to understand why I wholeheartedly felt that my life was "fucked up", given that circumstantially, it was actually very good. After all, I had abundant access to food, water and shelter; lived in a great neighbourhood; was surrounded by a loving, supportive family; was doing the thing I loved more than anything else in the world full-time; and the following year, I would return to studying commerce/law at Australia's most prestigious university. But when you hate yourself like I did – or in other words, when the most important relationship in your life – the one with yourself – is a disaster – then regardless of how "well off" you are circumstantially, your life will be a disaster too. And that, combined with the fact that I had no idea how to "fix myself" and finally feel well again, is why I kept on crying and crying, and why I felt so utterly hopeless.

Eventually, I staggered up, and with tears still streaming down my face, I drifted through the streets. I couldn't think of anything else but death. It's not that I – like most people suffering from severe depression – particularly wanted to die; rather, that I was just desperate to escape my torturous suffering, and dying seemed to be the only conceivable way. I imagined how soothing it would be. The answer to all my problems. Just blackness. Gentle, calm, soothing blackness. I fantasised about some of the different ways I could do it – like slitting my wrists in the bathtub, and then closing my eyes, leaning my head back, and waiting until I gradually drifted away. I thought about swallowing all the pills in my medicine cabinet, and then downing shot after shot of bourbon until I overdosed. I thought about trying to figure out where I could buy a gun, so that I could stick it in my mouth and blow my brains out. I thought about how I might be able to poison myself, hang myself, drown myself, gas myself … and then, I saw a bridge in the distance.

Feeling a surge of energy, I ran towards it. The closer I got, the less overwhelmed I felt, because in my suicidal state, the bridge was a salvation – like how I imagine land is to those lost at sea. I felt like I controlled my own destiny again. In a strange way I felt empowered.

When I reached the top of the bridge, I looked down – at the train tracks beneath it, and the bushy greenery on either side of them. And instantly, I felt a rush of disappointment.

The bridge isn't high enough, I remember thinking.

If I jump, then instead of dying, I'll get screwed by luck and just break all my bones.

Now that my salvation had turned out to be a mirage, I felt flattened by a brand new wave of anguish, and in that horrid, dangerous state, I pulled myself away from the bridge, lurched down the street, and stumbled into a bar.

'What can I get you?' the guy behind the counter asked.

I thought about how blissful it would be to taste the bourbon on my lips. To have it pumping through my veins before I melted into numbness.

'What can I get you?' the bartender repeated when I didn't say anything.

I wanted the bourbon so, so much – more than I'd ever wanted it before. But, I'd sworn to myself that after the Darling Harbour Night, I was going to stop drinking, and no matter how awful I felt, I couldn't stand the thought of giving in only a couple of weeks after making my pledge. So, in one of the smartest decisions I've ever made in my life, I ordered a Coke, sat down at a table, and then called my mum.

'Danny? Why aren't you at the writing course? Is everything all right?'

'No ...'

'Why?' she panicked. 'What happened?'

'Can you ... can you come and get me? Please?'

She left straight away, and was at the bar within the hour. By then, I felt completely exhausted, and it took all the energy I could muster to mumble to her what had happened on the way home. Once we'd arrived, I collapsed on my bed, curled up in a ball, and fell fast asleep until the late afternoon. When I was convinced I couldn't sleep anymore, I shuffled slowly into the dining room, and sat down with my mum on the couch.

'How are you ... how are you feeling, Danny?' she asked gently, taking my hand to hold between her own.

I sighed, and then shook my head – feeling so confused, so overwhelmed, so confronted by the morning's events that I had no idea where to begin.

'I can't ... I can't believe what happened today,' I eventually murmured. 'I can't believe how mad I was with myself ... and how I was crying non-stop for so long … and that thing about the bridge not being high enough to die … I mean that's just … that's just *so* messed up …'

I paused, and shook my head again as tears welled in my eyes.

'Something's wrong with me,' I finally said. 'Something's really, seriously wrong with me …'

Mum squeezed my hand.

'It's going to be OK, Danny,' she said. 'Dad, your brother Mathew and I are all here to support you, and tomorrow, we'll go to the doctor and make sure you get the help you need.'

She squeezed my hand even tighter.

'Just keep having faith, Danny. Whatever you do, you can't ever lose hope.'

*

The next day, I saw my general practitioner Dr Kramenin, and I told him everything.

'You're showing classic signs of clinical depression, Danny,' he said.

I remember being confused – in the sense that I hadn't heard of clinical depression before, and I didn't know what it was. That might sound crazy, but in 2009, it was even less talked about than it is now, and in my 20 years of living, I'd never come across it.

'Clinical depression?' I frowned. 'What do you mean?'

'Clinical depression,' he repeated. 'It's an illness, Danny.'

If anything, him saying it was an illness made me even more confused.

'What is it, exactly?' I asked.

'In lay man's terms, it's basically an intense state of unhappiness, experienced over a prolonged period of time.'

'But ... but doesn't everyone feel unhappy from time to time?'

'From time to time, yes – but not for prolonged periods. People with depression feel constantly miserable, often without relief. And the intensity of their despair is usually far greater than that experienced by a non-depressed person. Some people with clinical depression hate themselves. Some self-harm. Some kill themselves. Clinical depression is an illness, Danny, and it can be very serious.'

I nodded. The description fitted like a glove, and its recognition came with a wave of hope. *After all, if clinical depression is an illness,* I remember thinking, *then maybe there's some sort of "cure" that will help me overcome it ...*

'So you think ... so you think I've got clinical depression, then?' I asked, first wanting to make sure that that was indeed what I had. Dr Kramenin nodded, and then filed through his drawer before handing me a checklist called SPHERE, which was a scale he said was developed to increase the identification rate of mental illnesses like depression. I started reading it:

For more than TWO WEEKS have you:

Felt sad, down or miserable most of the time?
OR
Lost interest or pleasure in most of your usual activities?

If you answered "YES" to either of these questions, complete the symptom checklist below by circling the symptoms that are applicable to you:

Behaviours

Stopped going out;

Not getting things done at work;

Withdrawn from close family and friends;

Relying on alcohol and sedatives;

Stopped doing things you enjoy;

Unable to concentrate.

Thoughts

"I'm a failure";

"It's my fault";

"Nothing good ever happens to me";

"I'm worthless";

"Life is not worth living".

Feelings

Overwhelmed;

Unhappy, depressed;

Irritable;

Frustrated;

No confidence;

Guilty;

Indecisive;

Disappointed;

Miserable;

Sad.

Physical

Tired all the time;

Sick and run down;

Headaches and muscle pains;

Churning gut;

Can't sleep;

Poor appetite/weight loss.

I answered "yes" to "in the last two weeks have you felt sad, down or miserable most of the time"; and then circled "relying on alcohol and sedatives", "unable to concentrate", "I'm a failure", "I'm worthless", "it's my fault", "overwhelmed", "unhappy, depressed", "guilty", "disappointed", "frustrated", "miserable", "sad", "irritable" and "life is not worth living". After I was finished, I handed the test back to Dr Kramenin.

'You circled 14 symptoms,' he said. 'According to the creators of the test, you are likely to have a depressive illness if you circled at least three.'

Dr Kramenin then asked me a few additional questions, like whether I was also experiencing periods of mania or whether I'd had any hallucinations, for the purpose of ruling out whether I was exhibiting symptoms of other mental illnesses like bipolar disorder or schizophrenia. After being satisfied that I wasn't, he concluded that I was in fact suffering from clinical depression.

'So what happens now, then? Is there some sort of treatment I can undertake to get better?' I asked hopefully.

He nodded.

'Yes, Danny – I'm going to place you on an antidepressant medication.'

Once again I was confused.

'Medication? For depression? How can that be?'

'If you have depression, then it means you have a chemical imbalance in your brain – a deficiency of either serotonin, dopamine, adrenalin or noradrenalin. We use medication to treat depression in the same way we use medication to treat physical illnesses. There's no difference, really.'

I was shocked. I'd never heard of such a thing before. Then again like I've said, I hadn't heard of clinical depression before, either.

'I'm going to place you on a selective serotonin reuptake inhibitor,' he continued. 'This SSRI will increase the amount of serotonin in your brain, and thereby work to correct this chemical imbalance. You should feel better after that.'

He gave me a sample packet of pills and a prescription for more once the sample ran out.

Diary Entry: April 5, 2009

I feel so much better! Ever since I started taking antidepressants last week my brain has felt a hundred times clearer! My suicidal thoughts have vanished, and every day is so much easier without that voice in my head telling me that I'm a loser and a fuck up and a failure. I actually feel healthy again – probably as healthy as I've felt since the scholarship dinner all the way back in 2007. I'm so pleased! I know I've said this a hundred times before, but I really think I'm cured! I think I'm finally cured this time! All I needed was antidepressants! Now all my problems are solved and I can get on with writing my novel and trying to get it published by the end of the year!

One week later – mid-April, 2009

Hey Sylvia,

I feel so depressed again – almost as depressed as I felt on the day I went to the Writers' Centre – and I have no idea why. I mean, I've been taking my medication, but I think it's stopped working or something. So what am I supposed to do? How am I supposed to beat this illness? I keep thinking I've beaten it but I never have. I feel like I have no control over my brain anymore. I feel crazy.

I'm becoming really isolated as well. I don't want to talk to my friends anymore, because I don't think I'll have anything non-depressing to say to them. So don't worry about replying to this message or my last one. You must hate having to keep hearing about my problems all the time, so I'm going to stop dumping them all on you and just leave you alone. You're better off without me, anyway.

Danny.

She replied that same day:

Oh my God, Danny! Please don't think that you're dumping all your problems on me or that I'd be better off without you! Seriously, nothing could be further from the truth! I want to be here for you whenever I can because you're my friend, Danny. I care about you so much and I want you to keep telling me about what you're going through so that I can try to help if I can. So please don't ever forget that, OK? Seriously – thinking that you're dumping all your problems on me or that I'm "better off without you" is absolutely ridiculous! You're my really close friend and I'm here to support you and that's all there is to it.

That being said, Danny, I'm not a qualified psychologist yet, and I really think you need to start seeing one. I am only about to finish my second year of psychology at uni, but one thing my professors have really hammered into me is that just taking the drugs won't necessarily fix everything ... or anything. By adjusting your brain's chemical composition, the aim of medication is to reduce depression's intensity on a day-to-day basis – or as I like to put it, to help you "cope" with depression. But, the aim of therapy is to help you understand the underlying issues that are causing your depression, and then to treat those issues – which is what you need to do to actually recover and be free from depression in the long run. For example, usually one of the biggest reasons people are depressed is because of the way they think about one or more aspects of their life – and while medication can help those people cope on a day-to-day basis, what they really need to actually RECOVER FOR GOOD is cognitive behavioural therapy, which will help those people rewire the way they think in such a way that their new way of looking at things doesn't cause them to feel depressed. You see what I mean, Danny? So, I agree with your mum that you really, REALLY need to see a psychologist. Only then do I think you'll be able to conquer your depression once and for all and stop having so many relapses.

Apart from that, Danny, just keep hanging in there. You're so strong, and you can get through this – so just keep fighting, see a psychologist, and you'll beat your illness in the end. I know you will.

Love always,

Sylvia.

*

Everything Sylvia said was right, of course – particularly what she said about how medication only helps depression sufferers cope on a day-to-day basis, and that to actually recover and stop having relapses, what is needed is therapy (I've also learned since that if a person with depression can't afford therapy, then reading self-help books written by the world's most respected professionals can have a similar impact). But at the time, I didn't really understand the purpose of therapy, so instead of taking Sylvia-, her professors'- and my mum's word for it, I asked my GP Dr Kramenin.

'Do you think I need to see a psychologist? I've heard they can be really helpful – that sometimes the reason you're depressed is because of the way you think about certain aspects of your life, and that therapy can, among other things, rewire the way you think so that you can look at things in a way that doesn't make you feel depressed. What do you think?'

Dr Kramenin shrugged his shoulders.

'Danny, the reason why *you* are depressed is because of your situation – struggling at uni and battling to get your book finished. If you change your situation, then you won't feel depressed anymore – and for you, that means getting *Chrysalis* finished and doing well at uni. That's the key to you beating your depression.'

It's what I'd been thinking all along: *I've been depressed because I haven't been achieving my goals, so if I achieve my goals, then I won't feel depressed anymore.* To me, that line of thinking made perfect sense – *so what's the need to see a psychologist?* I scoffed. *I don't need therapy to "change the way I think", and in any sense, I've got Sylvia to talk through my problems with. Like she said in her last message, she'll always be there for me, so seeing a psychologist would be redundant. It would only waste time that could better be spent working towards achieving my goals, so it would actually do* harm *rather than good. So it's out of the question. No way am I going to see a psychologist.*

This was the first time – and unfortunately not the last – where I placed my faith in Dr Kramenin and he gave me awful advice that would shatter my life.

Halfway through the year, I was still having days where I felt depressed, worthless and suicidal, which almost always corresponded to days when I felt I hadn't achieved something I'd set out to achieve – like having a chapter of my book written by a certain point in time, or getting a High Distinction in the one subject I was currently studying at uni. But on the whole, I was feeling better than I did before the Writers' Centre Incident. Without a doubt, the antidepressant I was taking was one of the reasons why, because I'd definitely noticed feeling more stable and level-headed since I'd been on them. Not drinking had surely helped too – since I'd now been sober for four whole months. And, what had also been great was having been able to settle into a routine where I got to spend the majority of my days doing what I loved: writing. As usual, it filled me with abundant pleasure; and a peace that was so pure, so heavenly, so divine that I just wanted to continue doing it for the rest of my life. What's more, around that time, I also started discovering how cathartic writing could be, which allowed me to enjoy it on a whole new level, and which is why in the next draft of *Chrysalis,* so much of my own struggle found its way into it. For example, when my protagonist was living in a shanty town and battling to make ends meet, I made him turn to alcohol to escape. When he failed to reach the target amount of money that he wanted to make in a day, I had him falling into depression. At one point, I had him on the edge of a bridge about to jump. Hell, even the relationship between the protagonist and his lover started to mirror mine and Sylvia's, in the sense that it played a big role in helping him through his despair. Similar to the way journaling does, writing about my demons in my novel helped me release a lot of bottled up thoughts and emotions, and in an unexpected way, it also helped to keep me "on the right track". For example, when I was writing about how my protagonist overcame his alcoholism, it reminded me that I needed to stay committed to sobriety and not relapse. When I was writing about how he didn't jump off a bridge because he decided that he'd rather face his problems and beat them instead of running away, it reinforced the idea that I needed to stay strong and do the same. When I was writing about him achieving his dream at the end of the novel, it helped me remember that if I just kept working hard and never gave up, then I could also achieve mine. In this way, my protagonist became the man that I wanted to be. He helped give me strength, helped give me hope, helped me keep believing that my best days were ahead. He helped inspire me to keep on going.

By July, the next draft was almost finished. I planned to send it to Nick by the end of the month, and I hoped with everything in me that this time, he would say it was ready to submit for publication.

Dear Danny,

First off, I'd like to say that this draft is much, much better than your last one. You really brought the 1930's to life, and a lot of the silly schoolboy symbolism you used beforehand was eliminated. The ending was far less contrived. Good job.

However, I still feel you have a significant amount of work to do before you submit your book for publication.

Just like last time, Nick then went on to detail the problems with the draft. Firstly, he said that although my writing style had improved immensely, that the novel still wasn't as well written as it needed to be. Secondly, he believed the hardships that befell the protagonist occurred too close together, making large chunks of the novel too dark to be enjoyable. With regards to the main character falling in love with a black girl, Nick said that I still hadn't portrayed the "racial" issue anywhere near well enough. He also felt that the poetry still wasn't up to scratch.

Part of me was encouraged: *Nick says it's much better than my last draft, so that's obviously a positive sign. It's good that I've been improving, and because I'll continue working hard and I'll never give up, I have no doubt that one day, I'll have produced a novel that's worthy of being published.*

But on the other hand, I was worried about my dwindling amount of time.

I mean, what if I can't make all of these changes before uni starts? I fretted. *Then I won't get a High Distinction average, and then I'm going to be depressed, and then I'm going to want to kill myself again ...*

If I'd been seeing a psychologist and/or reading self-help books, then I would've been learning how *not* to think this way, and I would've been learning how to live a happy, healthy, depression-free life regardless of whether or not I finished my novel before uni started, and regardless of whether or not it ever got published. But since I still wasn't seeking professional help, my happiness was still almost wholly contingent upon achieving my goals, and in this way, I was a prisoner of my own unhealthy thought patterns.

Despite feeling as if I was in a race against the clock to get my book finished, I started getting involved in quite a bit of volunteer work in the second half of the year. In August, I did the 40 Hour Famine to raise money for World Vision, and in September, I signed up to participate in Movember, to fundraise for prostate cancer research and the mental health charity Beyond Blue. I guess I felt like I was doing my bit, but I really wanted to be doing more.

On many days, I'd find myself thinking back to the poverty I saw in Peru: the skinny kids wearing World Vision clothes; the 10 year olds selling cigarettes on the streets at two a.m. on a school night; and all the tiny homes that were made out of mud bricks. While I was there, I'd promised myself that I was going to continue contributing once I got back to Sydney, so while I was raising money for Movember, I also started looking into the feasibility of founding my own charity – to help the people I worked with in Peru and others like them around the world.

'But Danny, is now really the best time for you to be starting up a charity?' Mum questioned. 'It's a nice idea, but right now, you're suffering from depression, so you're hardly in the best place yourself. Don't you think it might be smarter to just focus on recovering for the time being, and then worry about helping others once you're 100% healthy?'

I shook my head.

'I am going through a hard time right now, yes – but eventually, I'm going to work my way out of it. I'm going to beat my depression. I'm going to be OK. But those kids ... they need people to help them. They're not in a position to be able to save themselves.'

I paused.

'I am in such a position to help them, though, and I don't want to put off doing so any longer. I want to help them now.'

I paused again.

'Every day those kids are suffering. When you look at it like that, I've already waited long enough.'

October, 2009

Over the previous few months – as had been the case for most of the year – I'd had good days and I'd had bad days, and on my bad days, I'd felt so depressed that I'd wanted to die. I figured that's just how my life would be until I achieved my goals, because it was when I was struggling to achieve them that I was sent spiralling into despair. With only one subject at uni at that point in time, my mood was basically pinned to my writing. If I felt like *Chrysalis* was on track to being finished by the start of the first semester of 2010, then I felt good. If I felt like it was still going to be at the draft stage, then I felt miserable, worthless and suicidal. In that way – despite how crazy it sounds – it wouldn't be much of an exaggeration to say that my life depended on getting my book finished by the 1st of March, 2010.

One thing that had changed lately, though, was that towards the end of the year, I started developing feelings for Sylvia. I knew we lived on opposite sides of the world, and I knew we'd been friends for years and that it was a dangerous line to cross – but all I could think about was how sweet, how tender, how supportive she'd been in my hours of need. No matter what I'd told her she'd always stuck by me, lifting me up again, giving me hope, and inspiring me to keep on fighting. She was the most compassionate, genuine, caring girl I'd ever met, and I found myself wanting to take the next step with her.

She was coming back to Sydney for two weeks after Christmas. My plan was to wait until she arrived and then tell her how I felt.

December, 2009

When I sent the next draft of *Chrysalis* to Nick, I felt really good about it. I was confident that I'd done everything I'd needed to, and that this time, Nick would finally say it was ready to be published. But all I could do was nervously wait and see.

In the meantime, a close friend and I founded a charity together! We called it the Open Skies Foundation, and once it was fully set up, we planned on funding projects that created sustainable change in Third World countries. Our first such project was going to be to build greenhouses in the villages I visited while I was in Peru, which would allow vegetables to be grown year-round instead of only three or four months a year. But unfortunately, we were still a while off from being able to fundraise for it, since there were a lot of burdensome and time-consuming legal and administrative hoops to jump through before we obtained the requisite license to do so. I hated having to wait, because the urge to make a difference burned so strongly inside me – particularly whenever I saw an old photo of one of those little Peruvian children wearing World Vision clothes. But, I knew I had to be patient, and focus on the long-term difference that I believed we could make. My co-founder and I had a clear vision, and we were dedicated to growing Open Skies so that one day, it would be operating in Third World call over the world. That was our goal: to change hundreds of lives across the globe. It was not a commitment for the next month, or the next year, or even for the next decade, but rather a lifelong pledge to help those less fortunate than ourselves.

Once again, it was those words that inspired me:

'Remember, Danny: to whom much is given, much is expected.'

At the end of our two week romance, we held each other in bed, and gazed into one another's eyes. I remember feeling sad, because the next day, Sylvia would be heading back to the States.

'What am I going to do without you?' I asked seriously.

She laughed.

'What are you talking about?'

I was thinking about how warm, how tender, how supportive she'd been through thick and thin. She was my rock, my saviour, and I couldn't bear to see her go.

'I'm going to miss you so much,' I said. 'Sydney won't be the same without you.'

'I'll miss you too. But we'll always have Facebook.'

Somehow, it didn't seem like enough anymore. Our two weeks together had been incredible, and I'd fallen head over heels for her. *How can we go back to talking only once or twice a week over the net?* I wondered.

'Maybe I could come and visit you sometime,' I said.

I expected her to be excited at the prospect, but instead, she just looked shocked.

'Huh?' she gaped.

'Well, I've never been to mainland America before. You could show me around. It would be so nice to see you again!'

She looked away.

'Uh ... well ... I don't know. Let's not think about it right now, OK?'

I looked into her eyes and smiled, still not sure what I'd done to deserve someone in my life as wonderful as her.

Life is fantastic! I just got my book review back from Nick, and he says that Chrysalis *is more or less finished! All I have to do is make a few changes, tinker with a few scenes here and there, tidy up the writing style a bit and I'll have a completed product! That's amazing! Particularly after everything I've been through! It's been such a long, slow, arduous process that's really tested my resolve, but I got there in the end and here I am – soon to be submitting my manuscript to agents and publishers! I can't wait!*

Uni's also starting in a couple of weeks. This year, I'm taking all third-year economics subjects, including all the honours stream ones. I'm not quite sure what line of work I want to pursue once I get into the corporate world, but I know it's definitely not law. In fact, that's why I'm taking the honours stream subjects – because once I've finished this year and earned my Bachelor of Commerce, I'm almost certain that I'm going to quit my law degree and do an honours year in economics, before applying to study a Master's of Applied Finance at Oxford, Cambridge or one of the Ivy League schools in the States. Honours in economics and then an MAF from one of the world's best universities will have me very well placed to get a job at a top tier management consulting firm, which is the industry that right now, I'm leaning towards entering. It all starts with this year though, and I want to smash a High Distinction average and finish my bachelor's on a high. And now that I've more or less finished my novel I'm primed and ready to do just that. Bring it on!

I feel like I'm in a really good place right now. For the first time since the scholarship dinner all the way back in my first year of uni, I'm really pleased with the direction my corporate career, my writing and my charity work is heading in, and that's something to really feel good about. Now that my goals are on track to being achieved, I feel like I'm back to my old self again – brimming with hope and confidence, and feeling happy and energetic and ready to take on the world. And my depression? That's long gone. Done, finished, kaput. Goodbye, you bitch. I've beaten you. You tried to break me but you couldn't, and right here, right now, begins the rest of my life without you.

PART III:

'THANK-YOU, DR GREGOR'

OR

'FUCK YOU, DR KRAMENIN'

On the first day of my Advanced Microeconomics Honours class, the professor ran us through the course outline and the assessment regime before delving straight into "game theory in extensive form". I'd arrived at the lecture feeling stable, confident and eager to learn the new material – but to my complete and utter shock, within 10 minutes I was horribly lost. I frantically tried to figure out what was going on while the lecturer continued.

'It is imperative to note the critical distinction between actions and strategies. Suppose player "I" in an extensive form game has "L" information sets: "I.1", "I.2" ... "I.L" etcetera, and that she has a choice of M_K actions at her "K-th" information set. Then, player "I" has "M_1" x "M_2" x ... x "M_K" strategies. If an agent has only one information set, strategies and actions are synonymous for that player. In particular, for a simultaneous-move game, the notions of strategies and actions coincide for each player.'

I was so confused. *What the fuck is he talking about? What the fuck is he talking about?* I started panicking. My notes were a mess – the professor was speaking far too quickly for me to get everything down. I scanned the room in distress, hoping to see everyone else just as baffled as I was … but to my dismay, all the other students were listening intently and calmly taking notes. I started berating myself.

What the fuck is wrong with me? How the fuck can I be the only person in the class who has no idea what's going on? How the fuck can I be so stupid? How the fuck can I be so dumb?

And the more I abused myself the less I could concentrate, and the less I could concentrate the further I fell behind. Throughout the two hour lecture I hardly absorbed anything, and during that time, my depression stormed back into my life and staged war on my mind.

Oh my God! I then started freaking out. *Oh my God, oh my God, oh my God! I thought I'd recovered! I thought I was cured! But I'm not! I haven't gotten better at all!*

I was fucking shaking.

Will I ever get over this? I continued panicking. *Is this just the way I am? Am I forever destined to a life of excruciating misery?*

By the time the class had finally finished, I was feeling so awful, so shocked, so terrified that I just wanted to die. In an attempt to rectify the situation, I anxiously took the bus straight home and forced myself to sit down at my desk and try to figure out the lecture material – but I was too depressed to be able to function. I took a break and tried again, but it was the same story all night long. Eventually, I gave up and tried to get some sleep, although I should've known there was no chance of me being able to just shut my eyes and drift calmly away. I was far too disturbed. I was far too horrified. I was in full-blown stress-out mode.

I just couldn't believe it.

How the fuck can it be back?

How the fuck can my depression possibly be back?

Three days later – March 7, 2010

Sylvia, where have you been? I'm going fucking mad here. My depression's back and I don't know what to do. What am I supposed to do? My doctor's put me on a stronger

antidepressant but it's not making any difference. Nothing is.
Fuck. Just please say something to help me, because I'm at a
total loss for how to fix this.
    Love Danny.

One week later – March 14, 2010

I was more depressed than ever. It had started on my first day back at uni
when I'd left class feeling like a failure; and had been multiplied by the
horrifying reality that I'd never in fact conquered my depression, and the
terrifying fear that maybe I never would. Feeling that depressed made it
difficult to study, so I fell behind at uni, which made me even more
depressed, which made it even more difficult to study, which made me
even more depressed ... and so the cycle went. The pain lasted for days at a
time, and during those days, I felt like a starving journeyman lost deep in a
forest, blindly wandering in the hope of making it out alive. The
journeyman has no food. He goes for three or four days, sometimes even a
week, without eating. Eventually he'll catch something, wolf it down – but
it's only a quick fix. Not long after he'll be famished again. Replace
hunger with depression and that was me. Food was my equivalent to all
forms of escape: T.V., reading and masturbation. They were temporary as
hell. Depression always prevailed.

During those days, I would think of suicide as much as the starving
journeyman would think of food. We had the same goal, too: get through
the day. Live until tomorrow. Just try to keep on going. Sometimes that
seemed too overwhelming, so I'd use the trick my addictions psychologist
had taught me two years beforehand, and break it down into smaller sub-

goals: *just survive the next twelve hours. The next ten hours. Hold off killing yourself until then.* It was so hard but I knew that I had to keep on fighting, I knew I couldn't lose faith that one day I'd get better. Every day I prayed: *God ... I am suffering ... I am drained ... please give me strength ... please give me the fortitude to beat this illness.* My life was such a disaster, but I had not abandoned hope – which is depression's fiercest rival, until one of them, always and inevitably, defeats the other. As long as I had hope I was in with a shot. As long as I had hope a way out was possible.

The next day – March 15, 2010

Sylvia, what's going on? I've tried texting you but you won't reply to my messages. Everything's so fucked up right now. I don't know how to beat this illness and I just keep getting worse and worse and worse. I'm so lost. So confused. Please help me. Please.

Five days later – March 20, 2010

I kept on floundering, kept on sinking. One night in particular stands out in my mind. It was three o'clock in the morning, and I was lying on my couch paralysed with anguish. I was in so much mental agony that it was affecting me physically, to such an extent that I was so heavy, so lethargic, that I could hardly move, hardly speak. Mum was beside me, clutching my hand. Tears were streaming down her cheeks.

'D-Danny ...' she sobbed. 'Danny pr-promise ... pr-promise me you'll never ... never k-kill yourself. OK?'

She clenched my hand even tighter.

'Do you promise?'

I managed to move my head, nod ever so slightly.

'B-because if you do,' she cried, 'then you might as well take me with you ...'

I knew I'd never do it. *No matter how much I want to die, I can't commit suicide,* I would always tell myself. *Suicide's quitting. Suicide's selfish. And I am not a quitter, and I'm not going to leave my family without a brother and a son.*

'Don't worry, Mum' I murmured. 'I won't.'

Two days later – March 22, 2010

Sylvia, what's with you lately? You never reply to texts, take ages to reply to Facebook messages, and you don't want to talk on the phone. Something about you seems so ... distant. Seems so foreign. It's like I ... don't even know you anymore. Seriously, Sylvia ... what's going on?

*

OK, Danny – maybe I have been distancing myself from you lately, but I have my reasons. You're depending on me more and more and ... look, I care about you, OK, and I want to be there for you – but you've got to understand that it's putting a hell of a lot of pressure on me. I'm only human, Danny, and I'm not a qualified psychologist either. I'm your friend, OK? I've been supporting you as your friend and I want to keep doing so, but you've got to realise that it can be very hard for me, particularly when all you seem to feel is depressed these days. You're not even seeing a psychologist, so you're depending solely on me – not to mention that your feelings for me are growing and growing and you're contacting me at rapidly increasing rates and ... I don't know. It's all just a lot of pressure, OK? It's scary. It's too much for me right now and I don't know how to deal with it.

March 26, 2010

We talked back and forth for the next few days, but everything ultimately came to a boil. Sylvia was feeling uncomfortable about the extent to which I was coming to her with my problems and about how attached I was getting to her, and once she aired those sentiments, I felt too self-conscious and uncomfortable to talk to her at all. So that was pretty much the end of it.

The timing also couldn't have been worse. As if I wasn't depressed enough already, I'd now messed things up with Sylvia – the girl I really liked, and the girl who was my biggest support system. I felt utterly, utterly devastated. I felt depression on top of depression. It was a whole new low that I'd never previously plummeted to.

In such a state, where I felt more distraught, more hopeless, and more bereft than ever before, I found myself thinking back over every attempt I'd made during the previous two years to beat my illness: trying to drink my way out of it; working myself to exhaustion at uni and on my novel; snorting cocaine in South America; working my ass off again on my novel and at uni; and depending on Sylvia for help and support.

And where has it led me? I asked myself. *I'm an alcoholic, suicidal on a daily basis, and I just lost Sylvia because I smothered her too much.*

There was no escaping the cold hard reality:

Nothing I have tried to beat my depression has worked. Every one of my attempts has failed.

I released an exhausted sigh before reality landed me another punch in the face:

I don't know how to fix my depression.

Admit it: I've got no idea how to fix my depression.

'Danny, will you *please* see a psychologist?' my mother begged.

I knew Dr Kramenin said I didn't need to, but I felt like it was my only option left. I was the most depressed I'd ever been, and I didn't know where else to turn.

'OK, Mum,' I nodded lifelessly. 'I'll do it. I'll see a psychologist.'

April, 2010

It took all the energy I had to heave myself out of bed and make it to my first appointment. I arrived at Dr Gregor's office feeling dreadful, and sat slouched in the waiting room with my head lulled lethargically back against the wall until he called me in. He was a tall, middle-aged man with brown hair, an unassuming posture and soft, gentle features. His handshake was prolonged, full of the warm familiarity of a mate, and his smile was broad and friendly, inducing me to reciprocate even though I felt horrendous. When he introduced himself he spoke in a calm, soothing voice and looked me earnestly in the eye. My immediate impression of him was that he was an amiable, down to earth bloke who wouldn't judge me no matter what I told him.

He led me from the waiting room into his office, where we sat down in comfortable arm chairs that faced each other. Then without further ado, I described to him everything I'd been through. For the longest time, I'd thought it would be difficult – opening up my soul and sharing my darkest, innermost thoughts with a stranger. But Dr Gregor was warm and non-judgmental, and even if he wasn't, I felt far too depressed to care what he thought of me anyway.

'And the worst part is,' I finally summed up, 'that I don't know what more I can do to beat my depression. I've worked so hard on my book and at uni but it's never enough. I always fall back into it. I keep thinking I've beaten it but it always comes back. I've tried everything to beat it but it always comes back.'

Dr Gregor frowned gently.

'I don't think that's true, Danny,' he said.

'You don't think what's true?'

'That you've tried everything you can to beat your depression.'

'But I have!' I insisted. 'During my first two years at uni I worked as hard as I could, but no combination of writing and studying worked to achieve my goals. Then I took a year off purely to write – I delayed my corporate career an entire year! – and that didn't work either. And now I'm back at uni and trying my best but it's still not enough. Nothing's changed. I've worked as hard as I can but I'm still so depressed.'

'That's not what I mean, Danny,' he said calmly.

'What do you mean, then?'

'In all the time you've been depressed – two years, now – have you ever once seen a psychologist?'

'Yes.'

'For depression?'

'No, for alcoholism.'

'What about for depression?'

'No.'

'Never?'

I shook my head.

'This is my first ever session.'

'Why didn't you see a psychologist earlier?' he asked.

'Because I didn't think I needed to. I thought that all I needed to do to beat my depression was to get a High Distinction average and get my novel published. I thought that after I'd achieved my goals I'd be happy again. That's what my GP's been telling me – that when I fix the situation I'm unhappy with I'll stop feeling depressed.'

Dr Gregor's eyebrows jumped.

'Your GP told you that?'

'That's what he always tells me.'

Dr Gregor shook his head.

'I don't think that's very good advice at all,' he said.

I was surprised.

'How do you mean?'

He sighed.

'Let me put it this way, Danny: what's going to happen if you *don't* achieve your goals? Are you going to be depressed forever?'

I flinched. It was such a brazen, confronting question.

'I ... I mean ... I th-think I will achieve them. But if I don't ... if I don't I'll ...'

'Even if you do achieve them this time round – even if you do get a High Distinction average this year and get your novel published – what about your next set of goals after that? What if you struggle to achieve those, just like you've struggled with uni and your novel? Does that mean you'll go through another huge bout of depression? And what about your goals after that, and the ones after that? Are you going to get depressed every time they don't go 100% according to plan?'

I was speechless. My whole world was crashing down around me. I was so sure that all I needed to do to beat my depression forever was to get a High Distinction average and get my novel published. That's what Dr Kramenin had always told me, and to me, it had always made sense. But the questions Dr Gregor was asking ... I'd never thought of them before. And now that I was, it seemed that my depression was destined to keep coming back, again and again and again, until the day I died. Consternation engulfed me. I was so scared that I literally wanted to puke.

'Yes,' I managed to croak.

Dr Gregor nodded.

'This is why the advice Dr Kramenin gave you wasn't very good. All he told you to do to fix your depression was to "change your situation", and as you can see, in your case at least, this would've set you up for a lifetime of relapses. Now, sometimes overcoming depression *is* as simple as changing your situation – but very often, the reason people suffer from depression is not actually because of their situation itself, but rather, because of the way they *think about* their situation. And this is what I think your problem is – one of perception, as opposed to one of circumstance. You feel suicidal every time you struggle or "fail", as you put it, to achieve your goals – and it doesn't have to be this way. My role as your psychologist will be to help you get to the bottom of why "failing" to achieve your goals depresses you so much, and then to help you perceive this "failure" in a healthy way that doesn't make you feel depressed.'

At the time, not getting depressed by "failure" seemed unimaginable. But, I tried to be hopeful.

'Do you really think I can get to that place?' I asked.

He nodded.

'If you commit yourself to therapy, then I'm confident you can.'

Our session eventually finished. I agreed to see Dr Gregor again at the end of the week, and we shook hands and parted. What he'd said sounded promising, but I just couldn't for the life of me ever envision a world where not getting a High Distinction average or my novel published didn't plunge me into a ghastly bout of depression. Hell, in the state I was in then, anything but depression seemed impossible to fathom.

April 14, 2010

The new medication Dr Kramenin had prescribed in response to my most recent bout of depression was giving me headaches, so he placed me on a different one yet again – this time, a relatively new drug that was part of the serotonin-norepinephrine reuptake inhibitor class of antidepressants. Mum was hysterical over it.

'Danny, you should *not* be taking that medication! In Beyond Blue's *Clinical Practise Guidelines for Depression in Adolescents and Young Adults*, it specifically states that for the type of drug you've been placed on, "further research is required before any conclusions can be drawn about its effectiveness and harms". For this reason, its use is *not* recommended for adolescents or young adults under the age of 24.'

'But Dr Kramenin prescribed it, so it must be OK,' I retorted.

'That does *not* mean that it's OK! All that proves is that Dr Kramenin hasn't read the guidelines!'

'He's the doctor, Mum! I'm not going to go against what he says!'

'I don't care if he's the doctor! You need to tell him to change medications again! You can't keep taking this one! You're only twenty-one!'

We argued about it for hours, and eventually, I was able to get my Mum off my back. She was still really worried, but the matter of my medication was just one too many things for me to deal with at that point.

For fuck's sake, I'm just trying to get through each day without necking myself, I remember thinking. *What medication I'm on is up to Dr Kramenin. It's his job to make sure I'm taking the right one.*

April 21, 2010

The days dragged along. This was the worst I'd ever felt. Period. There was no relief from the ceaseless dread. I could barely function. Paying attention in class was almost impossible. Studying was too overwhelming.

I'd fallen absurdly behind. I hadn't touched my book in days. I'd quit the job at the law firm I'd been working one day a week at as well – since I needed all my free time to try and catch up on uni. But there was never enough time. I was constantly exhausted. Drained of life. Depression sucked at my soul. My spirit withered. My goal for the day got broken down even further: *just survive the next six hours. The next four hours. Hold off killing yourself until then.*

I'd previously thought I'd get better. I'd always thought that hope and depression were bitter rivals until one inevitably defeated the other, and I'd always thought that hope would win out in the end. But for the first time in my life, I was devoid of hope. I honestly believed that being depressed was just the way I was, and that being depressed was just the way I'd be, for the rest of my life. And, because I was so convinced that I'd never get better, there seemed no point in fighting my illness. Instead of willing myself to "hang in there" because I believed that my suffering was temporary and that everything would be better one day, I comforted myself with the knowledge that human beings are not immortal. That I would die, one day. One special, glorious day. Then I could spend the rest of eternity mouldering in a grave, free from pain. You might be wondering why I didn't just kill myself if I wholeheartedly believed that my future consisted of nothing more than excruciating misery. Well, first of all, I still was not a quitter. But more importantly, I didn't want to hurt the people who loved me.

It's not fair to commit suicide and ruin their lives, I thought. *So I have to hold on. No matter how much it hurts me, I have to hold on* – which is why I drew comfort from the thought that one day I'd die and finally be free.

When you're that depressed, that insanely and utterly depressed that you genuinely believe you'll suffer that acutely for the rest of your days, life seems to lack all purpose. *After all,* I thought, *what's the point in working, fighting, striving for a better life if I'm sentenced to one of chronic anguish and despair? There is no better life. There is no life outside of pain. So what's the point in doing anything but waiting until death finally arrives on my doorstep and whisks me away to the Promised Land?* I was still studying, and I still planned on finishing my novel and trying to get it published – but it was more out of force of habit than anything else. My passion had been drained. My zest for life asphyxiated. I was like a ghost, just drifting through the ghastly days.

'Shit! What's wrong, mate?' an old friend said when I ran into him at uni. 'Perk up, brother!'

I was shocked. One of the most well-known attributes of depression is that it is entirely possible – and very common – to suffer horrifically without anybody knowing. But somehow without realising it, I'd crossed the line from a place where I was able to put on a front and fool people into thinking I wasn't depressed to a place where I was so sick that it was obvious to people I hadn't even seen for a year. When I got home I looked in the bathroom mirror, and realised that I was staring back at a young man whose eyes were exhausted slits, whose whole face shrieked of agonising misery. I was staring back at a young man whose spirit had been broken, whose soul had been destroyed. I was staring back at a young man who, for all intents and purposes, was already dead.

Three days later – April 24, 2010

I'd always taken a lot of pride in being a fighter, which in my books, meant having a tremendous work ethic; relentless determination; and most importantly, a never-say-die attitude. And, because I was a fighter, I'd always believed I could handle anything life threw at me, and that even though I might struggle and fall, I'd get up every time and succeed in the end. That'd been my MO, and that's what I'd always hung my confidence on.

But drifting through life a spiritless, broken shell of a man?

Giving up on happiness and resigning myself to a miserable, pointless existence?

Letting depression destroy the next 60 years of my life?

That's not fighting, I finally realised. *That's quitting. And that is* not *me. I'm not going to let depression break me,* I vowed. *Not now, not ever. I don't know when, I don't know how, but come hell or high water, I'm going to beat this illness, and go on to live a happy, healthy, fulfilling life.*

May, 2010

It took five weeks to understand the issue forming the crux of my depression – the "underlying issue", as Dr Gregor chose to call it. Over that time we were able to dig deep into my psyche, and after analysing my behaviour and the way I thought, Dr Gregor concluded that the primary culprit of my depression was a very unhealthy level of perfectionism.

'You relentlessly seek excellence, Danny, and you always set extremely challenging goals and then throw yourself into achieving them. Being perfectionistically goal-driven like this is fine in and of itself, but the problem with you is that you measure your self-worth entirely in terms of whether or not you achieve these goals. If you don't achieve a goal that you set out to achieve – like getting a High Distinction average or getting your novel published by a particular point in time – you hate yourself. You feel worthless and inadequate. You feel like a failure. And, you feel this pain so intensely that you'd rather be dead.

'You're human, Danny, and humans, by our very composition, are not perfect. Humans make mistakes. Humans don't always achieve their goals. You need to accept this, and not be so hard on yourself. You need to accept this, and be able to love yourself regardless. You need to be able to love yourself regardless of how you go in your uni exams and no matter what happens with your novel. Even if you fail every exam for the rest of your degree and your novel never gets published, you should still be able to love yourself. You should be able to find elements of yourself that you love that will be there no matter what. That will let you love yourself no matter what.'

He paused for a moment.

'If you can do this, then I think you'll go a long way towards conquering your depression.'

*

Over the next week, I tried really hard to find things I liked about myself that had absolutely nothing to do with achieving my goals. It wasn't easy for me, since like Dr Gregor had said, that's what my self-love had always been predicated on: if I was achieving my goals, or was on track to, then I loved myself; and if I hadn't, or was not on track to, then I hated myself. But, after a long time pondering, I'd finally written a healthy, outcome-independent list of things about myself that I liked.

I like that I'm a kind person – someone who always treats other people with respect.

I like that I'm an honest person who acts with integrity.

I like that I'm compassionate, and that I do volunteer work to try and help others less fortunate than myself.

I like that I'm a loyal friend, son, brother and grandson.

I like that I'm a good, supportive listener, and that I'll always be there for a loved one in need.

I like that I'm humble – in spite of everyone always telling me that I've accomplished a lot.

I like that I'm generous, and always willing to share what I have with others.

I like that I have the determination and the work ethic to pursue my dreams through to completion.

I like the fact that I'm a positive person. I like the fact that even after everything I've been though, I still feel tremendously blessed, still feel immensely fortunate to have everything that God has bestowed upon me. I like the fact that instead of thinking of myself as unlucky for having suffered such a severe depression, I think of myself as lucky for having all the support I'm getting to help me beat it.

I like that I'm religious – that I have God in my life to guide me and to keep me safe. I like it that I trust Him so deeply that I'm faithful no matter what.

I like that I'm a fighter. I like that I can handle everything life throws at me, and that even though I may struggle and fall, I have the strength to get up every time and beat it in the end.

And when I focused on those things, I could actually see that there really was a lot to love about me.

Wow, I actually am a good person, I remember thinking. *And this really is true –regardless of what my marks are at uni or whether or not my novel ever gets published. These are the reasons why I can love myself, and whether I succeed or fail doesn't compromise them at all.*

For the first time in a very long time, I was really able to see the good in me – and now that I could, I didn't feel worthless anymore. I didn't hate myself. I didn't feel inadequate. Instead, I felt confident, and proud of myself, and I didn't feel depressed at all.

*

I shared my psychological epiphany with Dr Gregor the next time I saw him.

'This is excellent, Danny,' he said. 'Measuring your self-worth entirely in terms of productivity and accomplishment is not healthy – but this – what you've just told me – *is*. And, combined with you taking your new medication which now seems to be working, I think it's the key to you overcoming your depression.'

Hearing that made me feel so empowered, so unburdened. But, it also made me feel a pang of unease.

'But Dr Gregor ... I *like* being a perfectionist,' I said. 'I *like* setting challenging goals for myself and then working hard to achieve them. Are you saying that it's not healthy to do that?'

He shook his head.

'Of course not, Danny. It's perfectly healthy to have goals and to pursue them passionately – so it's definitely something you should continue to do. But, it's critical that you love yourself – regardless of whether or not you achieve those goals.'

He paused.

'There are many, many good aspects of perfectionism. Like we've said, it obviously pushes people to strive for excellence and to reach their full potential. And in your case, I suspect it was the underlying reason why you never killed yourself. To you, suicide would've been quitting – the ultimate failure. And there is nothing, *nothing* a perfectionist hates more than failing.'

He paused again.

'It's a double-edged sword, perfectionism. The challenge for you, Danny, is going to be to retain the positives of it while banishing the negatives. And if you can remember and apply what we've talked about today, then I think you'll be able to do it. I *know* you'll be able to do it.'

May 22, 2010

Over the next week, at Dr Gregor's instruction I continued reading over my list – in order to help keep all of my healthy reasons to love myself at the forefront of my mind, and to continue embedding them into my subconscious. Each day, I'd read it 50 or 100 times, during random intervals when I had a spare few minutes – such as when I woke up; while I was waiting for a bus; in between classes at uni; or while I was taking a break from studying for my mid-semester exams, which just so happened to be around that time. Thanks to my work with Dr Gregor, I'd been feeling much better, and courtesy of a few all-nighters and some help from my friends, I'd been able to catch up on most of the work I'd fallen behind on. By the 22nd of May, I'd gotten the marks back for three out of my four subjects, and I'd done well – getting 80% for Monetary Economics, 88% for Advanced Microeconomics Honours, and 90% for Regression Modelling. I'd run out of time to properly catch up on all the material for Mathematical Economics, so I knew I wouldn't do as well in that one – but, I was hopeful I could scrape together 75%, and due to the other exams luckily being worth more, have my marks balance out to a High Distinction average.

The results were due to be released at 5:00 p.m. that day, so after reading through my list of healthy reasons to love myself a couple more times, I logged in to my university's online portal and went to the "Exams Results" section. As soon as I saw my score, my jaw dropped.

Nine out of 20.

Nine.

Forty-five per cent.

A fail.

I couldn't believe it. I'd never failed an exam at uni before. Never even come close. I was absolutely gutted. *Fucking hell,* I thought. *A mark like this is really going to drag my average down. It's really going to make it difficult to get a High Distinction average this semester. This is bad. This is fucked. Fuck, fuck, fuck, fuck, fuck.*

I stewed in disappointment for the next half hour before getting changed into my running clothes and heading to the gym. I popped into the bathroom before I went, and then while I was washing my hands, the magnitude of what had just happened hit me square in the face.

Wow! I actually exclaimed out loud. *I just got a shocking exam mark and I didn't abuse myself! I didn't call myself a loser and a failure and a fuck up! And I don't feel inadequate, worthless or suicidal! I only feel disappointed! Not depressed – just disappointed!*

I could hardly believe it. Before I saw Dr Gregor, an exam mark like that would've shattered me. It would've made me hate myself and wish I was dead. But now, all I felt was disappointment – a perfectly healthy emotion. *I've had a setback, yes,* I thought, *but that doesn't mean I'm worthless. It doesn't mean I'm a loser, a failure, or a fuck up. I'm still the same kind, honest, compassionate, loyal, supportive, humble, generous, determined, positive and strong-minded person I was before I received this exam mark; and instead of falling to pieces like I would have, I'll learn where I went wrong, do better next time, and then go on to live a happy, healthy, fulfilling life.*

Wow, I continued thinking to myself. *I never thought I'd say this on a day I failed an exam, but I actually feel great right now. I think I've finally conquered my demons! After all, God set me a huge test, and I passed with flying colours! In the past this would've completely destroyed me, but now I don't feel depressed at all!*

And there you have it, dear reader: a perfect example of how therapy can help you recover from depression. Rewiring the way you think and learning how to overcome your demons in this way is not something medication can do for you, or something talking to a friend can do for you, or something an online support group can do for you. Only therapy – and self-help books written by therapists – can help you get to the bottom of why you're suffering from depression, and then teach you the skills you need to climb your way out of it.

June, 2010

Thanks to Dr Gregor, I'd been feeling good over the previous couple of months, and to make matters even better, by the end of the mid-semester holidays, I finally finished *Chrysalis!* I'd finished making all of the little tweaks Nick had suggested, and it was ready to submit to literary agents! The way it usually worked was that you had to send them a one page "query letter" describing your novel, and then based on that, the agent might ask to read your manuscript, offer to represent you if they liked it, and then go on to present your work to publishing houses to try and get you a deal. It would be a long, involved process, and it all began with the query letter, so I started reading everything I could find on the internet about how best to write them – after which, I planned to write, rewrite and profusely edit my own. You could write a good book but if the query letter wasn't up to par then you wouldn't get anywhere, so it was well worth taking the time to get it right.

Aside from that, I was also getting ready to start the last semester of my commerce degree, and once again, I was aiming to get that so far elusive High Distinction average. I got almost 80% in the first semester, which, while disappointing, Dr Gregor had taught me to view as actually pretty good, considering how depressed I'd been at the start. That was something we were constantly working on – trying to get me to not be so hard on myself, to offer myself compassion, and to learn to think of things in shades of grey rather than so black and white. On the whole it was working, and like I said, on the whole I felt good. I could feel myself getting healthier and healthier – due to all the therapy I'd been continuing to do – and I was excited to embark upon my publication journey and jump right back into uni. I felt it was time to start a new chapter in my life – one where I was depression-free and ready to achieve my goals.

Despite me feeling well, though, my Mum was still very stressed out about the medication I was on.

'You shouldn't be taking this antidepressant, Danny! You're too young! Like I keep trying to tell you, it's not recommended for young adults under the age of 24!'

'Mum I'm sick of talking about this!' I'd retort. 'I'm doing well now – I don't want to change medications. And Dr Kramenin doesn't want me to, either.'

'Dr Kramenin hasn't read the guidelines! He's got no idea what he's doing! Don't you get it? Not enough research has been done on this drug to know its effects on young adults under the age of 24! You're like a guinea pig! Who knows what negative ramifications it might have in the future!'

'Dr Kramenin said it's fine.'

'Dr Kramenin doesn't know what he's doing!'

'Mum can you just drop it?'

'But Danny – '

'I said drop it, Mum! I told you – I'm sick of talking about this!'

Throughout the year, my charity co-founder and I had been working hard to get Open Skies off the ground. We were making progress, but unfortunately, we were still waiting on receiving the government's approval for our License to Fundraise, and until then, were forced to play the waiting game with great frustration. In the meantime, though, I'd started volunteering for 180 Degrees, which is a non-profit organisation that does pro-bono consulting for other NGOs. The first project I was assigned was to work closely with a charity that combatted violence against women. Broadly speaking, my team's role was to advise them how to achieve their objectives more efficiently, so we started breaking down the organisation into its various components and analysing where improvements could potentially be made. Just like the previous charity work I'd done, it was a very eye-opening experience, and in the same way witnessing Peru's confronting poverty did, learning about the heartbreaking plight of battered women shed even more light on just how lucky I really was, and further strengthened my belief that as someone who'd been tremendously blessed, it was my obligation to help those less fortunate than myself. Open Skies was my baby, my pet project, and as soon as we got our License to Fundraise I hoped to do incredible things with it – but in the meantime, I still wanted to do whatever I could to help others in need.

Unfortunately, things were still a mess with Sylvia. We'd tried to work through it but couldn't make any headway, and by September, we weren't speaking at all. It'd been bothering me, so I started talking to Dr Gregor about it.

'I think the problem with you two is that you had a very uneven relationship,' he said, 'and what I mean by that is that Sylvia was more your de facto therapist than your friend. You came to her with all your problems and she helped you through them, and the more this happened, the more you came to depend on her, the more emotionally attached you became to her, the higher a pedestal you placed her on, and the more you thought of her as some sort of "angel of healing" – and the more, I suspect, she thought of you as something along the lines of a mentally ill patient in need of help. It got to the stage where you became needy and started asking too much of her, and that made her feel pressured and scared and she started putting up barriers, and when that started happening, it bothered you to such an extent that you felt too uncomfortable to ever open up to her again. And the end result is that you're no longer speaking.'

I was confused – not about Dr Gregor's analysis of my and Sylvia's relationship, but about the general conclusion that it seemed to be implying.

'But then ... but then are you saying that it's not healthy to turn to a friend or a partner or whoever for support? Are you saying that it's healthier to just keep your struggle to yourself?'

He shook his head.

'Of course not, Danny. You never want to keep things bottled up inside you. It's good to talk to your friends, your partner and your family and to have their support, but when you have a mental illness, it's never good to rely on someone to such an extent that they become a *substitute* for a therapist – which is exactly what was happening with you and Sylvia. It's not good for the relationship as you've experienced, and it's also detrimental to you on a broader level – because when you have a mental illness and you rely on someone as a substitute for a therapist, then you're not getting the help you need. Love and support from the people closest to you is invaluable, but it can't take the place of professional help. It needs to be in addition to it, not as a replacement for it.'

He paused, looking at me carefully.

'Just think about it, Danny: if you had a physical illness or injury – a broken leg, diabetes or cancer, for example – you'd never refuse professional help and rely solely on the support of your loves ones to get through it, would you?'

I shook my head.

'No,' I said. 'Of course not.'

Dr Gregor nodded.

'Well, the exact same goes for mental illnesses as well, Danny. Nothing can take the place of professional help.'

I sighed, because I knew he was right, and because I knew that it was my own actions that had ruined things with Sylvia.

And, the saddest part was that such an outcome could've been avoided. It could've been avoided if I'd just gotten help from the very beginning.

With the end of my commerce degree rapidly approaching, I was thinking more and more about what I wanted to do in the corporate world, and I finally settled on management consulting. According to my classmates and all the recruiters from the top tier companies who were always visiting university, you basically got paid a ton of money to travel all over the world and consult on a multitude of fascinating projects. It sounded great – particularly the part about getting paid a heap of money.

That would mean I could live the life I've always envisioned! I thought excitedly. *I could own a big house on the harbour, have a couple of sports cars parked in the garage, and take my future family on overseas holidays every year! How cool would that be?*

There was no one path to take to become a management consultant, but after more and more thinking, I decided to do Honours in Economics in 2011, before applying for a Master's of Applied Finance at Oxford or Cambridge or one of the Ivy League schools in America. As for my law degree, I decided not to finish it. I found it dry and unenjoyable and it wasn't where my strengths lay. So, I applied for honours, and planned on quitting law as soon as I'd been officially accepted. But until then I had to focus on my bachelor's. My exams were only a couple of weeks away, and as always, I wanted to get a High Distinction average and thereby end my degree on a high.

November, 2010

How the fuck can this still be happening? I was panicking. *After all I've been through ... after all I've done to get better ... how the fuck can this still possibly be happening?*

I was suicidal again.

For the last five days of October and the first of November, I was horribly depressed, and what was most bewildering was that I had no idea why. Unlike before, my depression didn't seem in the slightest bit related to my perfectionism. Whenever I'd been depressed in the past, it was because I thought I'd failed at something, remember? I could always point to a "cause" – like a bad book review or an exam mark below 85%. But this time, there was no such cause. I'd just wake up and feel so miserable that I'd want to die. And for that reason, I couldn't use the techniques Dr Gregor had previously taught me to work through my despair. Being reminded of all the reasons why I ought to love myself wasn't working this time. Consequently, I was so shocked. So mind-numbingly terrified.

What the fuck is wrong with me now? What the fuck is wrong with me now? I continued panicking. *This year I've been doing all of the right things to recover and I really thought I had – so why the fuck do I feel the urge to kill myself again?*

And, with that horrified confusion came those petrifying questions – the ones that would nosedive me even deeper into depression and chill me to the bone.

Will I ever beat this illness?

Is this just the way I am?

Will I forever be condemned to a life of endless suffering and anguish?

Who knows? Who the fuck knows?

I wish I could just kill myself, I remember thinking. *I wish I didn't have any family so that I could just blow my brains out and nobody would care.*

*

Then the following week, I suddenly felt sublimely rapturous!

The days are so beautiful! I remember thinking. *I'm so lucky to be alive! God, thank-you for the gift of life! For giving me the senses to be able to see, smell, hear, taste and touch this beautiful planet that you've graced us with! Thank-you for blessing me with everything anyone could possibly want! And please help everybody who's less fortunate than me ... please help everybody who didn't wake up this morning feeling that today is a glorious gift from above!*

Wow! The world is just perfect! It's such a splendiferous oasis! Such a magnificent confluence of beauty – like Victoria Park next to uni! I love just strolling around and marvelling at the gorgeous green grass, smiling at the ducks in the pond, picking flowers off the jacaranda trees and twirling them hypnotically between my fingers, which is seriously like, the most beautiful thing in the world. And how about technology these days! I mean talk about incredible! The fact that we can speak to people on the other side of the planet is absolutely amazing! I was chatting to an old flame the other day and I was just thinking, "how are we not together?" Like seriously, we would be so good for each other! It's like that letter I sent her last year with the flowers, when I was talking about picking them all and laying them at her proverbial feet, and it just made so much sense, and it still makes so much sense, because I'll treat her so well, and she gets me, like we really, really click! I don't know what my brother's talking about, saying that it doesn't make any sense. He *doesn't make any sense! He doesn't understand how beautiful the world is! He doesn't understand how deliriously happy I am! Like, wow! This is the best I've ever felt in my entire life! I feel so invincible! So strong! So powerful! So indestructible! When I look up into the sky and sense the Lord's presence, it's like we're the same. I feel like God! I feel like God! I am so insurmountable that I feel like God!*

*

And then, I was depressed again.

I was depressed two days before my first end-of-year exam.

I was depressed two days after the most blissfully happy week of my life.

And I still had no idea how. All I knew was that I was so miserable; and so confronted, so frightened by my downfall that I wished I was dead. As usual, though, I didn't want to hurt my family, so instead of committing suicide, I tried to distract myself by studying for my exams, and through life's momentary pleasures like eating ice-cream, masturbating and sleeping (if I could manage to get it). But none of it ever worked for long. Depression always, *always* prevailed.

I really wish I didn't have any family, I couldn't help but think to myself. *Then I could just end it all and finally be free.*

*

Five days later, I was back to being high as a kite – feeling so energetic, so vivacious and so almighty again that I felt as powerful, grand and invincible as God. Dr Gregor said I was exhibiting classic symptoms of bipolar disorder – a condition where, when untreated, the sufferer oscillates between feeling extremely depressed and extremely manic ("manic" apparently being the unbridled euphoria I was currently experiencing). I seemed to fit the description, but psychologists provide therapy as opposed to diagnose mental illnesses, so Dr Gregor advised me to see a psychiatrist. I booked the next available appointment with the one he'd recommended, since I was desperate as hell to find out what was wrong with me. I felt so wildly unstable, so horrifically disturbed, and the "mania", if that's in fact what my highs were, was really starting to scare the shit out of me. I liked it at first – I think because I was just so relieved not to be depressed anymore. But after a while, it was just plain fucking scary.

I mean, feeling like I'm a superhero?

That I'm the greatest human being on earth?

That I'm as powerful as God?

Like what the fuck! I'd freak out. *That's just so ridiculous! I mean seriously, what the fuck is wrong with me? I'm crazy! I'm crazy! I'm literally fucking crazy!*

And the worst part was that I was actually aware of it. I *knew* that I'd lost my mind. I *knew* that I'd gone completely mad.

It was the most terrifying experience I'd ever had in my life – so much so that I genuinely preferred feeling suicidal.

*

And then right on cue, I felt like killing myself again.

I remember being outside in the sun, sitting around a table with some friends, and trying to study for my exam the following day. It proved to be somewhat of a distraction, but I could still feel my depression surrounding me, swarming me, suffocating me. I desperately hoped it would abate, but as the day wore on, it only grew more and more unbearable – culminating in the hour I had dinner with my parents at a small Japanese restaurant nearby. By that point in time, I was in so much mental agony that when Mum and Dad spoke to me, I couldn't talk back. I couldn't even look at them, couldn't do anything but sit there hunched in my chair, motionless, staring down at my plate. I hated for them to see me that way because I knew it was making them even more worried than they already were, but I couldn't help it. I no longer had it in me to appear cheerful and pretend that everything was fine. I was too drained. Too exhausted. There was nothing left but pain.

The next day – November 15, 2010

Woke up feeling ghastly. Dad drove me to uni for my exam. Silence all the way.

He dropped me off. I dragged myself to the exam room in a soulless, debilitated shuffle. When I got there I fell to the floor, sat slumped against the wall. My classmates talked to me, asked me questions, but still ... nothing.

We got called in.

'Ten minutes reading time, starting now,' the announcer said.

I tried to read. I understood the words on their own, but put together they made no sense. I flicked through the paper. Not much of it did.

The exam itself began. I reread questions I knew I'd studied for, but in the moment the answers were a blur. I felt like I was in a trance. The world seemed a black hole. A vacuum of suffering. I couldn't see any escape. The only possible salvation seemed death.

I scribbled down a few answers before the end of the test.

'How did you go?' one of my friends asked. But I just shook my head and shuffled spiritlessly away.

A couple of minutes later, I was outside. It was pouring down with rain. I had no idea what to do next. *Should I go home? Go to the library and study? Go to a coffee shop? Call a friend? Get smashed at a bar?* Every possibility seemed brutally unbearable. The only one that didn't was killing myself. In the past, I'd always thought that suicide was selfish, because even though it might've given me peace, I knew it would've left my family in ruins. But right then, on what was, unquestionably, the worst day of my life to date, I started to think that maybe I'd been wrong. I started to think that perhaps I'd been too narrow-minded.

Because I swear, I vividly remember thinking, *if my family knew how depressed I am right now ... if they could comprehend the gut-wrenching severity of the pain I'm in ... I swear they'd want me to put myself out of my misery. I swear they'd want me to end it all and finally be free.*

It was a dangerous revelation.

Does this mean I can die now? I thought. *Guilt-free and with my family's blessing?*

I stopped walking, let the rain pound down on top of me.

Can I do it? Can I really kill myself? Can I really jump in front of a speeding car and join the rest of the road toll casualties?

I stood at a right angle to the road, watched the cars zooming by.

Is this really it? Can I really end it all right here?

My mind was a warzone. So much conflict. But eventually, there emerged a definite answer.

No.

I can't do it.

It's the same answer I'd always reached, but this time, the reason was different.

It wasn't for me.

It wasn't even for my family.

It was for those less fortunate than me.

Regardless of how depressed I feel right now, I remember thinking, *I know that I've been tremendously blessed: with a loving, supportive family; with First World privileges; and with the opportunity and the ability to do whatever I want to in life. Regardless of how depressed I feel right now, I have had a lot bestowed upon me, and I have to use my good fortune to help others who aren't as immensely privileged as I am. If I kill myself, Open Skies will disband. All the charity work I'd planned on doing will never get done. I'd be abandoning all the people I have the capacity to help. And no matter how much pain I'm in I just can't do that. To whom much is given, much is expected. I can't kill myself. Not now, not ever.*

I felt it so strongly, with such paramount force that it couldn't be doubted. It was as if it was a calling, a message from God in my hour of need:

> *I put you on this earth for a reason, Danny. You can't leave it yet. There's so much that I've planned for you to do ...*

So I stepped away from the road. I called my mum.

'Hello?'

'Ma ...' I croaked.

'Danny? Are you alright?'

I murmured something inaudible.

'Danny?' she panicked. 'Is everything OK?'

'Come and get me ... please. From Wynyard.'

I met her there, crawled into the car, muttered in broken sentences what'd happened.

'Danny, we would *never* want you to kill yourself!' she stressed. 'Never, ever, ever, ever! Suicide is a permanent solution to a temporary problem! You know that, don't you?'

I eventually managed to nod my head. From the corner of my barely opened eye, I saw her fighting back tears as she tried to drive through the rain. At some point my father called, and she pulled over at a petrol station and stepped outside under the shelter to talk to him. I remained motionless in the front seat, curled up in a ball with both my eyes closed.

'Danny ...' Mum murmured when she re-entered the car. 'Danny we think ... we think it'd be a good idea for you to be admitted to hospital ...'

She paused solemnly.

'What do you think?'

I just wanted to get better. I was so tired of feeling sick and I just wanted to get better.

'OK,' I managed to say. 'OK. I'll go to hospital.'

November 18, 2010

Over the next couple of days, the necessary arrangements were made, and then on the morning of November 18, 2010, my mum drove me to a psychiatric ward just down the road from the hospital I was born in. It might sound strange, but on the way there, my spirits were lifted, and on the whole I felt hopeful. In hospital, I knew that I'd have frequent access to an excellent psychiatrist, be attending group therapy at least twice a day, and have a lot of free time to read self-help books – and I felt optimistic that as a result, I'd be able to get my life back on track.

When we arrived, I filled out some forms at reception, emotionally embraced my mother goodbye, and then took the stairs past the "Drugs and Alcohol Rehabilitation" unit on level two, then the "Eating Disorders" unit on level three, before reaching the "Mood Disorders" unit on the fourth and final floor. It contained a long corridor with about ten private rooms, five four-bed dormitories, a room for group therapy, a room to read and relax in, and two doctors' consulting offices. After being shown to my bed in one of the dorms, I unpacked my clothes, lay down, and waited pensively for my appointment with the in-house psychiatrist. If truth be told, I actually found myself hoping that she'd diagnose me with bipolar disorder – since while it's a serious illness, such a diagnosis would've explained why I'd been so disastrously unstable over the previous few weeks, and I was hopeful that with the right treatment for it, I'd be able to get better. Even if it wasn't bipolar though, I just remember wishing that I'd be diagnosed with something – because being in that limbo where I didn't know what was wrong with me, where I oscillated between feeling horrifically depressed and being mad as a hatter … I couldn't take it anymore. I was desperate for answers, and sometimes, anything's better than not knowing at all.

*

An hour later, I was introduced to a middle-aged, brown-haired, kind-natured psychiatrist called Dr Ravens, who then led me into one of the doctors' offices. Over the next 45 minutes I told her everything, and after asking me a number of questions, Dr Ravens concluded that I had "medicine-induced bipolar disorder". The bipolar part didn't come as a surprise at all, but the "medicine-induced" part was a hell of a shock.

'What do you … what do you mean, exactly?' I asked.

'I mean that the medication you were on had an adverse reaction with your brain, that unfortunately, has now led to you developing bipolar disorder.'

So it turned out that my Mum was right – I should never have been taking that particular medication, and Dr Kramenin should have never, *ever* prescribed it. In that moment, I finally realised that he was an awful doctor to be entrusted with treating my depression – particularly since he'd also previously discouraged me from getting therapy. I had every right to be furious with him, but to tell you the truth, anger was really the furthest thing from my mind.

What the hell, Danny! you might be thinking. *How could you not be mad at Dr Kramenin for all the incompetent advice he gave you? If that was me, I'd want to rip his head off! I'd want to fucking kill him!*

If that's how you'd feel, then I understand. But the way I thought of it, I'd just been told that I had a serious, life-threatening illness, and how I'd developed it was beside the point. What *was* the point, however, was learning everything I needed to about how to treat it, and then dedicating myself to doing all of those things. I knew that that was the only way I was ever going to get healthy again, and that feeling pissed off, bitter, sorry for myself or obsessing over how I could get revenge wouldn't get me anywhere. All of that negativity is just wasted energy, and the best revenge is always, *always* simply living well.

So with that in mind and only a few minutes left in our session that day, I asked Dr Ravens:

'Is bipolar disorder a permanent illness? I know that depression tends to be more of a "temporary" thing – in the sense that if you do the right things to combat it, then it can be overcome. But how long does bipolar disorder last for?'

I swallowed apprehensively.

'Is it something that I'll have to battle for the rest of my life?'

Dr Ravens met my eyes, and looked at me kindly.

'It's hard to say, Danny,' she said. 'Most people who have it do need some form of treatment for the rest of their lives. But in saying that, bipolar disorder is very manageable, and through a combination of medication, therapy and maintaining a healthy lifestyle, many patients become stable enough that they can live a happy, healthy life that isn't impeded by their illness.'

Late November, 2010

After five days at the psych ward, I began to feel immensely better. When I switched from the antidepressant I'd been taking to a mood stabilising medication, I stopped feeling suffocated by depression, and also stopped feeling wildly manic. For the first time in weeks I was on a fairly even keel, and I felt like I could think clearly again. Things were definitely looking up.

But in saying that, I found myself living in constant trepidation, because every day, I'd go to group therapy and see 30, 40, 50, 60 and 70 year olds tell the same old stories:

'I've been depressed for the better part of my adulthood.'

'My bipolar disorder has had me in and out of hospital ever since I was 25.'

'Mental illness is just a part of who I am. I've learned to live with it, but I know I'll never beat it. It will be with me until the day I die.'

Being in the psych ward made me realise that this was my biggest fear: being forever shackled by my illness. Not being able to live a normal life. Hell, just not being happy. I knew that I was willing to do whatever it took to recover, and I knew that I would never give up. *But,* I feared, *what if the balance of chemicals in my brain prevents happiness from ever being possible? What if my life is genetically predetermined to be a ghastly rollercoaster where I oscillate between insufferable depression and delusional madness? What if my destiny is this: a psych ward. I feel much better now, but how long will it last? Is a relapse through hell inevitable?*

But after ten days in hospital, I had my answer.

No.

My brain chemicals do not control my destiny.

I – Danny Baker – control my destiny.

Through group therapy, I learned a lot more about the 30, 40, 50, 60 and 70 year olds who'd been persecuted by their illness for decades of their life.

A lot of them drank.

Many of them were overweight, continued to eat unhealthily, and admitted to not exercising.

They had only tried a handful of medications.

They had only read one or two self-help books.

They didn't actively see a psychologist and never had for an extended period of time.

I was so surprised when I heard this. All I could think was, *how can they have such a serious illness and not do any of the right things to combat it?* At some point, I delicately asked as much.

'I saw a psychologist for a couple of sessions, but I didn't like it much so I stopped going,' one said.

'Self-help books are a bore.'

'I like eating junk food.'

'Exercise is hard work!'

'I've tried a few different medications. None of them worked.'

And the most universal conclusion:

'Depression is just a part of me. I've accepted it. It will never go away.'

I was flabbergasted. I couldn't believe it. I honestly felt like screaming:

'But guys! It doesn't have to be part of you forever! There are dozens of different medications on the market – how do you know that one of the ones you haven't tried won't work?

'You live in Sydney – there are dozens of different therapists here, and there are countless who work over the internet as well. You've tried a couple, but how do you know that another one won't be able to help you?

'What about all those self-help books? There are lots of them written by some of the best psychologists in the world! Millions of people have claimed that they've changed their life, so isn't it highly, *highly* likely that you'd also get a hell of a lot out of them?

'And eating healthily, sleeping well, exercising frequently and not drinking are the most basic principles of managing a mental illness. Don't you think you'd feel better if you abided by them?

'How can you just surrender yourself to your illness before you've thrown everything but the kitchen sink at it? There's so much you haven't tried – you've barely accessed any of the available help that exists! So you can fight it! You can beat it! Depression does not have to be your destiny!'

But I couldn't be so blunt. The most I could do was gently ask if one of those options may be of help to them. So I did. They shrugged. Someone then changed the subject and that was the end of it.

And that's when I reached the conclusion that I controlled my own destiny.

Depression and mania and psych wards do not have to be a permanent feature of my life, I realised, *because the means exist for me to conquer this illness. The means exist for me to be happy and healthy just like any other bipolar-free person, and if I do the right things, I will be. So, for the rest of my life I will eat healthily, exercise frequently, sleep enough each night, and never "cope" by drinking. I'll keep learning how to manage my illness by seeing my psychologist and reading self-help books; and while I currently feel stable on the medication I'm on, if at some point down the line I find myself struggling again, then I'll work with my psychiatrist to up the dosage or change medications.*

I'm not going to let this illness beat me. I'm going to fight it and fight it and fight it until I get better. I'm going to fight it and fight it and fight it until I'm happy again.

December, 2010

After two weeks, I left hospital feeling infinitely better than when I arrived, and ready to return to life a healthy, re-energised young man. I was looking forward to starting my honours thesis for 2011, and I couldn't wait to get back to submitting my novel to literary agents and working to get Open Skies' License to Fundraise. I felt good. Hospital was great for me – exactly what I needed. But, I never wanted to go back there again, and I planned on doing everything in my power to make sure I didn't.

PART IV:

LEARNING HOW TO BE HAPPY

January, 2011

Completely unforeseen to me, at the start of the new year, my Economics Honours application was rejected, because it turned out that I hadn't done one of the pre-requisite subjects. It was never clear that that subject was mandatory – after all, it was a zero credit point *law* subject – so I spent days sending emails all over the faculty trying to talk them into letting me do honours regardless, or at the very least, letting me do the pre-requisite subject concurrently with honours. But, they weren't having a bar of it.

'Rules are rules,' they said. 'You'll just have to wait to do honours in 2012.'

Wait a whole year? Are you fucking kidding me? I thought. *All for a zero credit point law subject that couldn't be any less related to economics?*

It was exasperating. Uni-wise, I'd had exactly what I wanted to do mapped out, but this technicality had completely ruined my plans. I was furious, but since there was nothing I could do to change the faculty's mind, I frantically set to work trying to figure out what to do with the year instead – and for lack of alternative options, eventually resigned myself to just completing my law degree.

It definitely wasn't ideal at all, since I'd wanted to quit law, remember? For months my plan had been to do honours in Economics, and then study a Master's of Applied Finance before going on to become a management consultant. But I knew that a law degree would open the same doors for me, since many of the skills you learn studying law are also useful for management consulting, and if it meant not delaying my corporate career another year, then I preferred to just suck it up and finish it over the next two years, even though I didn't like it very much.

No matter what, I cannot delay my corporate career another year, I convinced myself. *All the scholarship holders I started uni with are about to finish their law degrees and enter the work force, and I'm already a year behind them because I took 2009 off to write – so I can't fall behind anymore. I just can't. Therefore, I have no choice – I* have *to study law. I wish I didn't have to but I don't have a choice.*

February, 2011

By this point in time, I'd ideally loved to have been signed by a literary agency – but unfortunately, the agents I'd submitted my query letter to in September and October had rejected me, and due to having been so sick, then going to hospital, then studying for and resitting the exams I'd missed, and then having to sort out all the drama at uni, I hadn't resumed since. On the bright side, though, one agent in particular gave me some valuable feedback on the start of my manuscript – she said that she didn't like my use of a prologue to open the novel, and recommended a few other ideas. I wasn't sure I agreed with her, and I knew my mentor Nick was a big fan of the prologue, but I'm always open to constructive criticism, so I was experimenting with her suggestions before I got back to querying other agents. To date, the process hadn't gone as smoothly as I would've liked, but I remained optimistic. After all, there were still dozens of agents I hadn't yet queried, and I was tightly crossing my fingers that one of them would want to work with me and then go on to make my dream come true.

March, 2011

I'd been working hard to get Open Skies off the ground, but we were still stuck trying to get our License to Fundraise. The relevant government department was stretched so thin that it was taking forever. They'd receive our application, take three months to review it, ask for additional information, take another three months to review that, then ask for even more information, etcetera, etcetera, etcetera. It was a frustrating process, but I was hopeful we'd be granted our license soon and then be able to get to work.

In the meantime, I was volunteering with a few other organisations. I'd begun doing a second stint with 180 Degrees Consulting – this time doing pro bono work for a charity that was combatting sex trafficking in South East Asia. The second NGO I was working for was the Australian League of Immigration Volunteers (ALIV for short), who help refugees in community detention. In January I volunteered at their holiday camp, where we spent a week taking children to the beach, theme parks and other fun places to brighten up their day, and since then I'd been involved in ALIV's monthly weekend program where we did the same thing. Thirdly, I'd been visiting an online mental health forum to lend an ear to sufferers who needed someone to talk to, and to offer them the support of a person with first-hand experience of what they were going through. It was all so eye-opening, and like charity work had always done to me in the past, it hammered home just how lucky, just how immensely and richly blessed, I really was.

I mean how else can I feel, I remember thinking, *when I hear stories of thousands of girls as young as five or six being sold into prostitution by their very own families? How else can I feel when I hear about them being tortured, beaten unconscious or having a bucket of live snakes or maggots dumped on them as "punishment" for fighting back when a violent client tries to rape them? Or about how some of them get infected with AIDS and then die before they're 20?*

Then there were the refugees. *How can I not feel tremendously grateful for the education I've received when I do reading practice with a 15 year old boy from Sierra Leone who can't pronounce the word "football"? How can I not feel even more grateful for being raised in a nurturing, peaceful country like Australia when every afternoon at camp, an eight year old boy from Iran begs me to sit with him by the Parramatta River and silently gaze at the soothing, tranquil water because it "relaxes" him? Or when I meet a child who's fresh off the boat from a war-ravaged country, but whose family didn't make it to the Promised Land with him?*

And then of course there was everyone I'd speak to who had a mental illness, and it was those people, more so than anyone else, who made me realise just how good I really had it. *How can I, of all people, not feel inexpressibly lucky when I talk to teenagers who are suicidal, manic or psychotic, yet whose parents "don't believe in mental illnesses" and thus refuse to get them help? I mean fuck, these kids were* me *last year! Particularly the ones who have bipolar disorder – they're as unstable, suicidal and deluded as I was. But my parents had been supportive. They had been kind, and loving, and had gotten me the help I so desperately needed.*

And that got me to thinking:

Where would I be right now if I hadn't had anyone to help me? If my parents were like these kids' parents and had said that mental illness was a farce and that if I didn't snap out of it they'd kick me out of home?

I certainly wouldn't have recovered, so they inevitably would've thrown me out.

There's no way I could've held down a job being that sick, so where would that have left me?

Homeless?

Probably.

And what does life hold in store for a homeless young man who's gone completely mad?

Nothing.

Except death.

In other news, I'd resumed submitting my book to literary agents – but then I stopped again after rereading my favourite novel *Candy,* since it had led me to think of an exciting new idea.

In the same way that Candy *explores the lives of two lovers trapped in the throes of a heroin addiction, I could write about something analogous that's centred around mental illness. If there's one thing I know it's depression, and I think I could draw on everything I've been through to write a really engaging fictional story that in addition to thoroughly entertaining people, also raises awareness about depression and reduces the stigma surrounding it.*

But, I also knew that this new story idea would overlap with the depression-related aspects I'd inserted into *Chrysalis,* and that for that reason, I could probably only ever release one of them. Obviously, *Chrysalis* made the most sense to pursue since I'd already written it, but the way I saw the plot of my new idea unfolding, I really, *really* believed it could be a masterpiece. *And, if I can only publish one book,* I remember thinking, *then shouldn't I go all in on the very best one that I'm capable of writing?*

I wasn't 100% sure what to do, so I decided to hold off submitting *Chrysalis* to literary agents and just take my time and think.

*

Around this time, while I was fantasising about different novels I could write and the awareness I hoped to raise about depression and mental health, I simultaneously found myself getting more and more bored studying law. I was giving it my best shot, but every day, I'd be forced to sit through hours of lectures that I couldn't have cared less about.

'The identification of the ground of judicial review is contingent upon which remedial model is applicable. Under the "common law remedial model", the overarching question is whether an error which gives rise to a particular ground of review can be classified as a jurisdictional error, because some remedies (specifically, prohibition and mandamus) only issue for such errors. If it cannot, the error may still attract a remedy (i.e. certiorari) if it is an "error of law apparent on the face of the record".'

Oh who gives a fuck? I couldn't help but think. And every time that sentiment shot through my mind, I couldn't help but wish that I didn't study law. I couldn't help but wish that I wasn't forced to do something that I'd never liked to begin with and was starting to despise.

But I'm trapped, I wholeheartedly believed. *I don't have a choice, I don't have a choice. I wish I didn't have to study law but I don't have a choice.*

I kept going back and forth on what to do with my writing. Like I said, sometimes I thought I should just continue with *Chrysalis,* because I'd spent three-and-a-half years writing it and it would be a waste not to. But most of the time I thought I should go with my new idea, because I really believed it was a much better concept.

To help me decide, I met up with my mentor Nick to talk it over.

'*Chrysalis* is a good book, but it's not a great book,' he said. 'But this new idea … this new idea could really be something …'

It was confirming what I already believed to be true, so with titillating excitement, I set aside *Chrysalis,* and in the coming days began writing what would ultimately become *I Will Not Kill Myself, Olivia* – and I was having a blast! Whenever I'd start I'd get so absorbed in the plot, so enveloped in the characters' lives, so lost in my imaginary world that I'd never want to stop. I knew I had to be careful, though, since too much writing and not enough studying is what had gotten me into trouble during my commerce degree. For this reason, I made a rule that I could only write after I'd finished all my law readings for the day – which I thought would prevent me from repeating my previous "mistakes".

Another thing I thought it would do was give me some extra motivation to actually finish those law readings – which was something I desperately needed, since lately, I'd been falling behind in class. I'd really been trying my best to keep up to date, but whenever I'd study, I'd just grow so bored, so frustrated, so unhappy that eventually, I'd get fed up and stop. There genuinely wasn't a single thing in any one of my subjects that interested me, and while I'd never enjoyed law to begin with, after studying it full-time for the previous few months, I'd truly begun to hate it like hell.

In the past, it had taken me by surprise. It had shocked me to my core. It had seemingly come so out of the blue that I hadn't known what had hit me. But this time, it was almost expected.

It was back.

That harrowing despair. That anxious dread. That feeling that life is so overwhelming, so insufferable that I wished I was dead.

Depression.

This time, my relapse was the consequence of having to do something I hated, hour after hour after hour, day after day after day. Every time I'd sit down to study, I'd psych myself up by reminding myself of why I was doing so: to graduate with a law degree, which I knew would help me get a job at a top tier management consulting firm. For the first several pages of my readings, that motivation would be able to sustain me … but then, I'd get bored, and my mind would start to wander, and then I'd get frustrated for not being able to concentrate, so then I'd try to refocus, but then it would happen all over again, and again, and again, and then I'd just want to scream *I fucking* hate *studying law! I hate studying law so fucking much!* But like I said, I'd convinced myself that I had to and that there was no way out of doing so. And, when you feel like you're trapped in a life you hate, it's only a matter of time before you start to feel depressed, and then it's only a matter of time until you start thinking about suicide – because your depression has convinced you that it's your only escape.

A week before the end of semester exams – when I could only manage to study for 20 minutes before I'd feel so miserable that I'd want to slice my wrists open – I mentioned how unhappy I was to my mum, and that I thought it would be a good idea for me to go back to the psych ward so that I could get some more help.

'That sounds like a good idea, Danny,' she said. 'If you think you need to go back to hospital, then I think you should go.'

She paused for a moment, looking at me seriously.

'But, I also think you need to stop studying law.'

I flinched.

'W-what ... ?' I stuttered.

'If it's making you this depressed then you need to quit.'

I was speechless.

'I can't ... I c-can't do that,' I finally stammered.

'Why not?'

'Because ... because I need a law degree to get into a good management consulting firm.'

'What about an honours degree?'

'What do you mean "what about an honours degree"? I couldn't do honours this year. I hadn't done that pre-requisite subject, remember?'

'But you've done it now, so why don't you just quit law and do honours next year – which is what you wanted to study all along anyway.'

'But I can't!' I cried. 'I can't delay my corporate career another year! Don't you get it? All the scholarship holders I started uni with are already a year ahead of me, so I can't fall behind even more! Therefore, I *have* to finish law. I don't have a choice!'

'Of course you do, Danny. You always have a choice.'

'No I don't – '

'Yes you do, Danny. You always have a choice.'

Over the next few weeks, I spent a lot of time talking to my parents, with the aftermath being that I decided to quit law and do honours in 2012 instead. Mum, Dad and Dr Gregor helped me realise that I do in fact have choices in life, and that it's a mistake to travel a path that isn't right for me – which studying law definitely wasn't. So, I dropped it, and as soon as I did, I stopped feeling depressed – particularly since I also came to be at peace with the fact that I was delaying my management consulting career another year. That was the other thing my parents and Dr Gregor helped me understand – that I had to go through life at my own pace, instead of constantly comparing myself to other people like the scholarship holders and thinking that I'd "fallen behind", or that I was inferior to them in some way if I wasn't "advancing my career as quickly as they were". They helped me understand that what everyone else was doing with their life was irrelevant, and that all I should be concerned with was trying to find my own path, and being the happiest Danny Baker I could be.

It was a period of realisations for me. As anyone who knows me will tell you, I'm a diehard NBA basketball fan, and around that time, I started thinking a lot about something that the Oklahoma City Thunder coach Scott Brooks had said:

'Even though we finished third last in the league in 2009, the whole year I was telling my guys, "we're not losing games ... we're learning how to win them".'

Over the next two years, the young Thunder continued to get more experienced, and after a while, they began to reach their potential. In 2011, instead of finishing 28th in the league, they finished in the top four, and made it all the way to the Western Conference Finals.

"We're not losing ... we're learning how to win."

I loved the inherent positivity behind that quote, and loved its implication that as long as the Thunder were learning as they lost, they would inevitably start winning. The notion struck a chord with me, and it got me thinking about my own mental health.

I could say a similar thing about my illness, I concluded. *Instead of thinking of myself as suffering from depression, I could think of myself as someone who's learning how to be happy. I'm learning how to be happy because I'm learning to understand myself better. I'm learning what triggers those plummets into despair. I'm learning how to pick myself back up again whenever I do take a plunge. And, I'm learning valuable life lessons from my parents and my psychologist that I'll carry with me for the rest of my life. In this way, it's as if there's a fortress surrounding my brain that's there to protect me from getting depressed, and every time I learn a bit more about how to be happy, another armed guard gets posted outside it. Sure depression's army still gets through from time to time, but that just means there aren't enough guards defending it yet. But, if I keep on learning how to be happy, then – combined with diligently taking my medication, eating well, sleeping well and exercising frequently – I'll eventually have so many guards protecting me that depression's army will be shut out for good. It'll have no way of getting through.*

If the team stays together, then I think it's only a matter of time until the Thunder win the championship.

Just like I believe it's inevitable that I'm going to beat my illness.

*

The corollary to quitting law was also that once again, I got to spend my days doing what I loved more than anything else in the world: writing. Compared to law – or to anything else for that matter – it's hard to describe the pleasure writing gave me. I remember trying on numerous occasions to articulate it, but I was never able to come up with a perfect explanation. The best I could do was say that, when I was writing, and when I really lost myself in it, I felt as if I was transported to a different place. All my pain just melted away, and I felt at peace with the world. I felt blessed to be alive. I felt more blessed than ever to be me. I felt a pulsing rush ... of excitement, of joy, of inspiration, all at the same time. I felt invigorated. I felt alive. I felt free. And above all else, I felt happy. Purely and utterly happy.

Towards the end of the year, 180 Degrees announced its first ever international consulting project, in partnership with a grassroots organisation in Cambodia that ran programs supporting children who'd been victims of abuse, parental neglect, human trafficking, or who'd been orphaned. I was fortunate enough to have been selected as part of the team, and in December, we were set to start looking at ways in which the organisation could better achieve their long term objectives, before flying to Cambodia in February to work closer with them and help out on the ground. I was really looking forward to meeting the team and starting the project, and also to doing hands-on volunteer work again like I'd done in Peru. Open Skies was still in the process of getting its License to Fundraise, and until I could really get going with that, I relished the opportunity to support other charities.

At the start of the month, I sent the first draft of *I Will Not Kill Myself, Olivia* to Nick, and while I was waiting for him to read it, I began doing some preparatory work for honours the following year – like revising a lot of the bachelor's degree material that I'd need to know, and doing some early research for my thesis. I wanted to get a head start, because my goal for honours was to get the university medal.

It would sure do wonders for my corporate career! I remember thinking. *If I was able to get the medal, then I'd be almost guaranteed to get accepted into one of the best universities in the world to study a Master's of Applied Finance, and then, I'd be in a prime position to get a job at a top tier management consulting firm. The upside is so big that I have to go for it. I have to do whatever it takes to try and get that medal.*

Economics was my forte – I knew I could do it. But, I also knew that I'd have to be more dedicated than ever. To average the required 90%, I'd need to have a near-perfect mastery of the subjects, and I'd also need to write an outstanding thesis. It was doable, but there was no margin for error. I knew I'd need to study really, *really* hard. I knew I'd have to put absolutely everything I had into it. I knew I'd have to go for it to the exclusion of almost everything else.

But then that got me thinking, *what about my writing? When am I going to get a chance to write my novel if I'm working 12 hour days busting a gut to get the medal? These last six months have been incredible – being able to dedicate myself solely to the thing I'm passionate about. I've always known it wouldn't last, and that I wouldn't be able to write anywhere near as much once uni started – but the way honours is shaping up now, I don't see how I'm going to have time for it at all. And, if I can't write – if I have to shun the thing I love – then how will it be possible for me to be happy?*

*

The tension continued to mount in my troubled mind.

I really want the medal for all the doors it will open, but how can I not write for a year? I'll be unhappy if I don't write for a year, but given my corporate world goals, I won't be able to live with myself if I don't go for the medal, either. So what am I supposed to do?

Balancing life's competing priorities like work, family, friends, hobbies, exercise, relaxation, travel, volunteer work and spiritual devotion is something a lot of us struggle with, and finding the right harmony is one of the essential ingredients to good mental health. At its core, it requires you to have the self-awareness to be able to answer one very, *very* important question:

What makes me happy?

And at that point in my life, I still wasn't able to answer it. I knew I wanted to do what was best for my corporate career, and I knew I wanted to do what was best for my writing, but both options seemed mutually exclusive. My "balance" seemed destined to become completely lopsided the following year, and there seemed to be no way to keep it at a stable equilibrium. Consequently, I felt as if I was destined to once again feel depressed, and in anticipation of feeling depressed all through 2012, I started feeling depressed in the present as well. And as was so often the case, my suffering triggered the urge to drink. I started having those nights again where I was clutching my hair on the edge of my bed, sweating through my clothes and panting through gritted teeth as I desperately tried to fight off the cravings. Usually I wouldn't give in, but on one occasion the pain was so overwhelming that I thought *who gives a fuck if I have a drink?* so I went out and had over 20. I stumbled home and wanted to keep on drinking, so I opened the liquor cabinet and got another bottle to take to bed with me.

'Please put it back, Danny,' my mother pleaded, her hands nervous and shaking as she reached for the bottle. 'Please, please put it back.'

'I need it, I need it!' I stressed as I backed away from her. 'Don't you get how much I need it?'

'Danny I'm begging you!' she cried, staring at me wide-eyed. 'Please put the bottle back! *Please,* Danny!'

It was such an ugly scene that I eventually did so out of guilt, but that didn't stop the cravings, it didn't stop the pain ... and that's why all of a sudden, I started experiencing the insatiable impulse to cut myself. I remember just wanting to get a steak knife from the kitchen so that I could rip it through my flesh. I remember wanting to slash up my arms and watch the blood spurting out, just so that I could feel something different from craving booze, just so that I could feel something different from depressed, just so that I could distract myself from the voice in my head telling me that I'd never be free from my illness so I might as well kill myself. I know it sounds sick, but just like drinking, self-harm can serve as an escape, because when you're in intense physical pain, you temporarily forget about your even-more-intense mental pain. And I wanted to forget, I wanted to forget, all I fucking wanted was to forget ...

The urges were so, so strong – to drink, to cut myself and to kill myself. But, I knew that drinking was a mistake, I knew that cutting myself was an even bigger mistake, and I damn well knew that killing myself was the ultimate mistake. No matter how overwhelming the desire, I knew I couldn't give in. I knew I had to keep on fighting.

Hang in there, I'd keep on telling myself. *Don't give up. Trust in God, he knows what's best.* Having been in such a position before, I knew I could get better. But, I also knew that it would take work to do so. I knew that what I needed was to take a time-out from everything and resolve the conflict that I needed to resolve.

So, I arranged to go back to the psych ward.

November 21, 2011

My parents drove me there, and they waited in the reception area while I checked in, before hugging and kissing me goodbye with tears in her eyes. Then, just like last time, I walked upstairs to the "Mood Disorders" unit on the fourth floor, and after unpacking my things in my room, I saw my psychiatrist Dr Ravens. As she usually did, she asked me a myriad of questions, and then afterwards, she decided to prescribe an additional medication for me to take on top of my current one. It was likely to help stabilise my mood, but I knew that I couldn't just rely on the drugs. I knew that – through therapy and by reading self-help books – I needed to put in the work myself, and learn how to think in a healthier way, or make changes in my life that would lead me to be happier. I knew that only then was I actually going to get lastingly better, and go on to achieve my ultimate goal of living a happy, healthy, depression-free life.

*

For the first few days after I started taking my new medication, I was too tired and drowsy to do much. But on my fourth day, I was feeling much more alert, so I took Dr Gregor's advice and started reading a self-help book by Dr Martin Seligman called *Authentic Happiness*.

And, by page 14, I'd learned everything I'd needed to to work my way out of my despair. It's why I believe with all my heart that self-help books written by the world's most renowned professionals are the most underrated – and underutilised – tool people have to fight their depression, and why I believe with all my heart that every single person who struggles with depression should make reading them a part of their day. Just like therapy, they can give you the insight you need to be able to understand what triggers your illness, and they can teach you everything you need to do to overcome it.

And the best part? They're affordable for *everyone*.

*

On page 13 going on 14 of *Authentic Happiness*, Dr Seligman speaks of doing activities that leave us feeling invigorated, and of doing activities that leave us feeling drained. If my interpretation of the text is correct, what he's basically saying is that you will have greater happiness in your life if you do *more* of what leaves you feeling invigorated, and *less* of what leaves you feeling drained.

The idea resonated profoundly with me, because it so perfectly characterised how I felt after writing and studying economics. Writing left me feeling inspired, and exhilarated, and completely alive. But studying economics – even though I found it somewhat interesting – would leave me feeling mentally exhausted. It would leave me feeling like a flogged horse, and afterwards, I'd just want to read a book, or go to the gym, or play basketball, or go out with my friends, or do anything else that would let me clear my head and get away from it. Consequently, what Dr Seligman said made me wonder, *what would the rest of my life be like if it was full of pursuits that left me feeling invigorated – i.e. writing – instead of pursuits that left me feeling drained – like studying economics and presumably the corporate work to follow?*

And that's when I had my epiphany:

I would be happier if I spent my life writing novels instead of studying economics or working as a management consultant.

It was an extraordinarily powerful realisation, because I'd never contemplated the idea of writing for a living before. I'd only ever dreamed of just publishing the one novel, and since I was 16, I'd dreamed of getting rich through a lucrative career in the corporate world. But thanks to Dr Seligman's self-help book, my entire outlook on my future had changed. By the end of the day, I was no longer an Economics Honours student/budding management consultant who was writing a novel on the side – rather, I was an aspiring author, who studied Economics Honours so that I could be a management consultant if I couldn't make it as a writer. I still wanted to have that back-up plan in place, because I didn't want to end up a "starving artist". But, I was going to prioritise trying to make it as an author, which meant that in 2012, I wasn't going to stop writing to focus 100% on getting the university medal. Instead, I was going to continue working on my novel, and study just enough to get the minimum marks required to be accepted into the least competitive post-graduate school that I wanted to attend (75-80% instead of 90%).

With that issue resolved, the balance in my life was back, and as a result, I didn't feel depressed anymore. On the contrary, I felt excited, and inspired, and elated over my newfound epiphany, and at the pro

trying to make a living as an author. I couldn't wait to get the hell o

hospital and dive headfirst into it.

I stayed in hospital for another week, but it was really just to keep an eye on things, just to play it safe more than anything else. Like I said, I stopped feeling depressed as soon as I'd had my revelation, and a week later, I was discharged feeling great.

Will I ever have to come back here? I remember thinking on my way out.

I hoped not. The lesson leading to my epiphany was one more very important one that I knew I'd take with me forever, and I hoped that – combined with everything else I'd learned over the years I'd been suffering from depression and bipolar disorder – it would be enough to prevent another relapse in the future. To use my "war metaphor" again, I hoped I now had enough soldiers surrounding my brain to hold off depression's army from ever attacking me again. But, only time would tell whether my defences were strong enough. Until then, I was focused on Nick's review of the first draft of *I Will Not Kill Myself, Olivia*:

> *Dear Danny,*
>
> *In summary, I think this draft is a great start – the best writing I've seen from you so far. This novel is bold, raw and confronting – nothing is left at home – and the fast, edgy writing style suits it well. The whole notion of depression/suicide is also very topical, and it's an area of life that has not been understood. It's also a recurring theme as we look at the psyche of the post-modern world: why are so many people unhappy when we're better off, materially, then at any time in history?*

But as with all first drafts, there are things that need fixing in the second. For starters, the opening chapters of the book are not up to par, because you don't do a good job of setting the scene. Manly in Sydney is one of the most beautiful places in the world, but you wouldn't know it from the way it's currently portrayed in your novel. You need to paint the picture properly – make the reader feel how magical of a place it is. See my notes on the attached manuscript for ways to do this.

Aside from the opening, I thought there was much to admire in the first half of the book. It was easy to read; had good character development; some great insights; and most importantly, it felt real and authentic. I was rooting for Jimmy fighting against all the odds and got caught up in his story – until about the halfway point, when I started to find the plot too dark and introspective. The personal anecdotes, day-to-day events and the characters that have leavened the story up to this point have run out, and then, it's just Jimmy's depression. I think people will be interested, then fascinated, but will then feel that it's too harrowing. You want to take them out of their comfort zone, yes – and you do a very good job of doing so – but you don't want to hold them hostage.

You have created an excellent basis for a great fictional story, but to make it really exceptional, you are going to have to weigh it right. This is the tricky thing about such a dark journey – especially one that is rooted in reality. You need to get the right balance between light and dark, between informing and entertaining. Again, see my notes on the

manuscript for how to do this – particularly in the second half
of the novel.

Great work, keep it up.

Nick.

The other awesome piece of news I got that month was that after almost two years, Open Skies finally got its License to Fundraise! I was so happy, and I couldn't wait to start helping the communities we'd chosen to work in. In Peru our first project was to build greenhouses like I said, and we'd also set up a project in Cambodia, where we planned on paying instructors to teach disadvantaged women how to weave hand-made products from natural resources, which they'd then be able to sell in hotels and local markets. We couldn't wait to start fundraising for both of them, and within a week of receiving our license, we'd already planned exactly how we were going to do so in 2012.

At the end of the year, I felt like I was in a really good place. My writing was going great, and Open Skies was finally ready to go! I was doing what I loved, and not surprisingly, I felt the best I'd felt in years.

PART V:

EAT, PRAY, LOVE: THE YOUNG ADULT'S VERSION

OR

STILL LEARNING HOW TO BE HAPPY

In the interests of working on my novel and raising money for Open Skies, I delayed thinking about my honours thesis as long as it was wise to. But, when the new year began, I started feeling the pressure to come up with a topic.

'You need to make sure you pick something you're passionate about,' the course co-ordinator said. 'You'll have to spend the majority of the year working on it, so you'd better make sure it's something you're really interested in.'

I had a look through all of the recommended topics: twenty-first century fiscal policy; post-GFC government regulation; labour laws and the European Union; all the chaos that was happening in Greece. None of it appealed to me, so I then started researching more obscure topics: happiness economics; the economics of time; something about speed limits and accidents and politics. None of it excited me either, so I pushed my thesis to the side and returned to hustling up donations for Open Skies and moving forwards with *I Will Not Kill Myself, Olivia*. The money was rolling in for our projects; and the paradisiacal setting of my novel was starting to come to life, as I worked at painting Manly's idyllic picture, and capturing the sunny, blue-skied beauty of the great Australian outdoors. It was all going wonderfully, but after another week, I knew that I really needed to stop for a while and get back to my thesis.

Over the next few days, I did some more research to try and come up with a topic, but I just couldn't find anything that I was passionate about. After I'd looked into practically every branch of economics there was, my mentality turned from *I need to find a topic that I'm passionate about* to *I just need to do whatever will get me a good mark*. With that objective in mind, I spoke to a friend who'd done honours the previous year and had absolutely aced it.

'I did my thesis on microfinance,' he said. 'My supervisor was amazing, and if I was you, I'd just pick a topic in that area and let him guide you. You'll kill it if you do.'

So that's what I ended up doing.

'What in the area of microfinance interests you?' the supervisor asked when I met up with him.

I shrugged.

'Is there any chance that you could just choose a topic for me? Maybe something that *you* find interesting?'

He considered this for a moment.

'I'm currently focusing a lot of my research around competition and microfinance,' he said. 'How about something to do with that?'

I shrugged again.

'Yeah. Why not?'

'OK, well in that case, how about I give you some journal articles to read? You could have a look at them and come up with a more specific topic yourself, and then, I could guide you from there.'

So that's what I started doing, plodding through journal article after journal article: *Competition and Microfinance; Competition and the Performance of Microfinance Institutions; How Rising Competition Among Microfinance Institutions Affects Incumbent Lenders; Microfinance in Times of Crisis: The Effects of Competition, Rising Indebtedness, and Economic Crisis on Repayment Behaviour; Microfinance Trade-offs: Regulation, Competition and Financing; Competition and the Wide Outreach of Microfinance Institutions;* etcetera, etcetera, etcetera.

And within the week, depression's army had blown past my soldiers and staged war on my brain again.

To my grave dismay, I realised that I was about to begin an honours course that I was no longer interested in. I'd started my thesis and looked over the course work, and all it did was bore me senseless.

I didn't know how this had happened. I'd thought I wanted to do honours. I'd thought I'd enjoy it. But it was all just so dry and uninspiring compared to writing my novel.

'I think you'll just have to suck it up for a year,' my parents said, 'because you need to do honours if you want to become a management consultant.'

That then led me to start thinking about what it was going to be like to be a management consultant, and that's what had ignited depression's assault. For the first time, I wasn't focusing on the big fat dollar signs – on the harbour-side mansion, the sports cars and the overseas holidays. Instead, I was finally looking at it for what it really was.

Management consultants help organisations improve their performance.

And, just like honours, it didn't inspire me at all. If I ever needed a reminder, on my second day of being in Cambodia that month for the 180 Degrees Consulting project, I met a man called Tok who'd been forced to fight in the Khmer Rouge against his will. One day, when he went to get some food during a break from training, a landmine went off in front of him. He fell unconscious, and when he came to, he realised his arms were gone.

He said he wanted to kill himself.

'There was no future for me,' he confided. 'What could I do? How could I get a job, get married and support a family without any arms?'

There was a grenade in a bag attached to his waist. He arched his body around and tried to reach it, so that he could pull out the pin and end his life. But, his friend saw him just in time and took the grenade away.

Tok was then taken to hospital, where he stayed for the next nine months. When he eventually left, he was too embarrassed to go back to his family and rely on them for help, so he started begging on the streets.

Months later, Tok's mother found him and took him home – but before long, he had to return to the capital city for more treatment. He then used up all of his money on hospital bills, and ended up back on the streets again.

Luckily, an aid worker soon found him, and he was given a job selling local crafts and gifts to tourists who were visiting Angkor Watt. He then fell in love, got married, and had two children. Now Tok runs his own business, selling books at a stall in Siem Reap.

'I'm very happy now,' he said.

I took his contact details, since it was such an incredible story that I had the thought of writing his biography once I'd finished *I Will Not Kill Myself, Olivia*. It was a story that the world should hear, and I thought I could use some of the proceeds to pay for his ongoing medical bills and to put his children through school.

That was the kind of thing that excited me: meeting incredible people, writing incredible stories, and giving back to the world. That's what got my juices going. That's what made me feel truly alive. But helping billion dollar organisations improve their performance? That did nothing for me.

'But you can write in your free time after work,' my classmates said.

That was what I used to think too, before I took off the money goggles and really thought things through. Then I was asking myself, *when will I have the time to write, to really try and make it as an author, if I'm working 60, 70 hour weeks?*

'But you only get pushed that hard in your first five or ten years,' my classmates rebutted. 'It all eases up after that.'

I wasn't convinced that was always true in practice, *but even if it is,* I thought, *how am I going to have time to write when I'm over 30 and married with kids, even if the hours have reduced to around 50 a week?*

I'd worked so hard for one of those jobs without really thinking about it, because I thought all the money would make me happy. At a top tier management consulting firm, you make close to six figures in your first year out of uni, half a million after 5-10 years, and in the vicinity of a million after 10-20. Financially, you've got it made. You're as secure as can be. But now I was finally looking at the work for what it was, and the idea of putting in 60+ hours a week to help organisations improve their performance made me want to shoot myself.

As a result, I was self-destructing. I was exploding at the seams.

For fuck's sake! I remember panicking. *The career I've worked so hard for is actually a nightmare! Another one-way ticket to the psych ward and a life of depression!*

I felt so unstable, so uncertain, so vulnerable, so terrified, and consequently, I felt so horrifically suicidal. The urge to run away, to quit, to buy a gun and put a bullet through my head was stronger than ever before.

But, I knew that I wasn't going to do that. Unlike in the past, I knew exactly what my problem was, and what's more, I knew exactly how to fix it. The only question was whether or not I had the courage to do it.

I mean fuck ... can I really abandon my back-up plan – my guaranteed, lifelong financial security for myself and my future family – to instead chase some crazy artist's dream?

The questions kept coming as I desperately tried to ward off depression's onslaught. *Can I really ditch my back-up plan? Can I really bail on management consulting after all these years? Can I really put all of my eggs in one basket and try to make it as an author? What about my financial security? What about my mental health?* I was locked in turmoil. For days I kept going back and forth and back and forth, racking my brain trying to work out what to do. It helped to have someone to talk it over with, so like I'd been doing most nights, I Skyped my mum on the other side of the world.

'If I work a corporate job, I know I'm going to be depressed. I know that it's sensible to have a back-up plan, and I know that management consulting is a great one from the standpoint that I'll make a lot of money. But what's the point if it's just going to make me suicidal and send me straight back to the psych ward? The reason I've always fought like hell to recover in the first place has been so that I could get another crack at life. It's been so that I could get another chance to be happy. And working 60+ hours a week in a job I'll hate, just to make a lot of money, just so that I have a back-up if I can't make it as an author, is hardly giving myself a chance to be happy. But going all out with my writing, throwing myself into the thing I love and doing everything in my power to make a life out of it ... *that's* giving myself a chance. *That's* listening to my heart. *That's* following my own path like you and Dad say I should.'

I'd never articulated such a sentiment before. Just hearing myself say it ... it was so obvious what decision I needed to make.

'So that's what I'm going to do,' I said. 'I'm going to forget about management consulting and just give it my all to try and make a living as an author.'

'I think that's really wise, Danny,' Mum agreed. 'Dad and I both believe that you have to do whatever you feel is going to make you happy.'

I knew Mum and Dad would be supportive. A lot of parents might object to their son throwing away a safe corporate career to chase a wildly unpredictable one, but my parents have never been the kind to pressure me into living the life that they want for me instead of the life that I want for myself. While they've always given me advice, they've at the same time left those decisions up to me, and given me the freedom to go after my dreams. They never had any fixed ideas about what job they wanted me to have – they just wanted me to be happy and healthy. And, if that meant bailing on management consulting and pursuing creative writing, then that's what it meant.

I kept talking to Mum.

'So,' she said. 'Do you think you'll be able to make it as an author?'

I'd thought that question over a thousand times that month, and I knew exactly what my answer was.

'Yes,' I said confidently. 'I really believe I can make it, because I know I have the right attitude to make my dreams come true: I have a tireless work ethic; relentless determination; and I never, ever, *ever* give up. I really believe in the novel I'm writing, and even though it's not ready to be published yet, I know that in time, it will be. It's inevitable that it will be, because I'll keep at it and at it and at it until it is.'

'I believe in you, Danny, and because you have a good attitude, I have no doubt that you'll eventually have a manuscript that's worthy of being published. But, you still need a bit of luck. After all, what if the agent reading your query letter is having a bad day and they just gloss it over, assume your novel isn't worth publishing like the other hundred books being pitched to them, and then pass on it? What if the only agents that would be interested in representing you don't have the time to take on new clients? What about that interview you told me about when an agent actually admitted to at times requesting to see manuscripts based on the author's *initials*?'

She sighed.

'Like you've often said, Danny, there's just *so* much luck involved … so what if it doesn't fall your way?'

I'd thought a lot about that over the last month, too.

'That part's up to God,' I said. 'I trust Him.'

*

So, I quit honours, and as soon as I did, depression's army retreated, and the war was over. It had taken a lot of hard work – a lot of self-analysis to understand myself better and to work out what I really wanted out of life – but like I've said, that's all part of learning how to be happy. In that respect I'd taken a huge leap forward, and as a result, I felt so liberated, so inspired. Instead of dreading my future, I was now looking forward to it with unbridled excitement.

This is incredible! I remember thinking exuberantly. *I mean, I actually have the freedom to chase my dream! How amazing is that?*

I felt so elated. So overjoyed. I couldn't wait to fly back to Sydney and start my new life.

March, 2012

When I returned home, I started telling my friends that I'd scrapped my back-up plan and was going full tilt to try and make it as an author. To be honest, I didn't expect them to understand. I thought everyone would think I was crazy for abandoning what many consider to be the Holy Grail of professional careers to chase one that's so risky and uncertain. I thought I'd get heaps of 'what the fuck were you thinking's and a myriad of starving artist jokes. And of course I got some. But to my surprise, a lot of people thought what I was doing was really cool. And to my even greater surprise, some people even seemed ... envious.

'I wish I could do what I'm really interested in too,' one of my mates said. 'I'd really like to be a journalist, but instead, I'm working 80 hour weeks at a law firm.'

'I'd love to go to the Caribbean for a year and be a scuba diving instructor,' another friend said. 'But now I'm working six days a week as a management consultant.'

'I've always dreamed of going to a little village in Africa and doing hands-on work for an NGO. Instead I'm working as an investment banker, and I don't even like it. I really wish I could just do what I enjoy.'

'But you *can* do what you enjoy,' I said. 'You guys are only 23 – you're still so young! If you want to be a journalist, then be a journalist. If you want to be a scuba diving instructor, then be a scuba diving instructor. If you want to work for an NGO in Africa, then work for an NGO in Africa. Now's your chance. Go for it!'

They all just stared at me, shocked, unable to say anything.

For the first month after I'd quit honours, I'd wake up every day and just write, write, write, completely smitten with my brand new life. By then the next draft of *I Will Not Kill Myself, Olivia* was finished, so I sent it back to Nick – feeling confident that I'd successfully taken on his feedback and produced what would be close to a finished product. I knew it would take him 4-8 weeks to review it, so I then got a job at a call centre to make some quick cash in the meantime. Accordingly, I spent the first two weeks of April sitting at a desk with nothing but a phone and a thick stack of paper, dialling up strangers all over the country.

'Good afternoon, may I please speak to Steve?'

'Speaking.'

'Hi, Steve! My name's Danny, I'm calling on behalf of Charity *XYZ*. How are you today?'

'Oh ... good, I guess.'

'That's good! Look I'm just calling for a quick catch up, can you spare a couple of minutes?'

'Yeah make it quick.'

'Of course! So I'm calling for a couple of reasons – firstly, I'd just like to extend a *huge* thank-you for supporting Charity *XYZ* in the past! It's because of people like you that we can help local and overseas communities, so thanks a lot for that!'

'OK.'

'And if I may ask, do you remember what *inspired* you to give your support in the first place?'

'No, it was a long time ago.'

'No worries! And have you had a chance to keep up to date with the work we've been doing lately?'

'No not really.'

'That's OK! So look you may be aware that Charity *XYZ* plays a vital role in times of crisis and emergencies that affect thousands of people around Australia. I'm sure you've heard all about the Queensland and Victorian floods, for example?'

'Yeah.'

'Now Charity *XYZ* is committed to helping communities as disaster strikes, and thereby enabling victims to rebuild their lives. For example, *over $16 million* was paid out to households damaged in the Victorian floods! But even though great work is being done, thousands of people are still in need. Your support would make a big difference, Steve, so what we'd like to do today is kindly invite you to re-join us as a Regular Giver and help transform the lives of thousands of people in need. Does this sound like something you might be able to do today?'

'No not today sorry.'

'That's alright, mate. Well nonetheless thanks a lot for your support in the past, and best of luck for the future.'

'Thanks, bye.'

I'd then write down the time I called Steve on a piece of paper, circle "NEGATIVE" next to his name, put it in the ever-growing "REJECTED" pile, and then dial the number on the next piece of paper.

It was so wearisomely tedious, so mind-numbingly boring, having to repeat the same thing over and over and over again, in the same fake upbeat tone, always putting emphasis on the same old words. Then there was my supervisor always breathing down my neck, demanding that I put more pressure on the person to donate: *'you can't let them off the hook so easily'; 'you've got to rephrase the way you ask them'; 'you've got to sweet talk them more'*. Blah, blah, blah. It was awful. The whole time I was on the phone I'd be watching the clock – literally – just willing the time to pass faster. And then at the end of my second week, on the long bus ride home at half-past nine at night, an anxious fear took hold of me as the cold hard reality set in:

My novel isn't published.

I'm broke as fuck.

I don't have a girlfriend.

I'm 23 years old and I live with my parents.

I spend my days working a mundane, minimum wage, dead-end job that I hate.

It had all started off so romantically – writing all day without a care in the world. When I was doing what I loved and when I got on a roll, it was easy to see myself succeeding; it was easy to envision myself in the future as a published author with bestsellers to my name and a loving, supportive family by my side. But working at the call centre had given me a preview of my future if I never in fact made it:

> *I'm 40 years old and living in a one bedroom shithole downtown. I'm still working mundane, minimum-wage, dead-end jobs during the day to scrape by while I bust a gut writing all night – only to see my manuscripts get rejected again and again and again. I'm still single – after all, what do I have to offer a woman? – and when anyone thinks of me, it'll be as someone for whom life held so much early promise, but who in the end amounted to nothing. They'll all say, 'Danny Baker – what a gigantic waste'. And the worst part is that I'll agree with them, and that I'll be plagued by that thought every day of my life.*

And on that particular night, exhausted after another horrendously monotonous eight hours at work, the only future that seemed possible was the one where I didn't make it. All I could see myself amounting to was that lonely, unfulfilled, miserable man and it scared the shit out of me.

The next day

Dear Danny,

I can see that a lot of work has gone into this draft, and while the second half of the book is now less dark and you've made an obvious effort to bring the love story more to the fore, there is still another draft required.

For starters, the opening couple of chapters of the novel still aren't up to scratch. Again, you need to do a better job of setting the scene, and on second reading, I also think you need to develop Jimmy's character better in these chapters too. We need to know Jimmy's thoughts and feelings earlier on so that we know what's driving him – so that when he falls into depression later on we understand exactly why. Right now we learn the reasons too late – by which time, the reader has started questioning the character and doubting his authenticity. So you need to beef the start up a lot. Slow it down, set the scene more, insert more segments here and there to allow us to understand Jimmy earlier.

Like I said in my last report, the middle of the book is in good shape and has some very powerful sequences, but I still think the second half of the story could be structured better. While it's less bleak now, some of the interplay between Jimmy and Olivia is a bit repetitive, and a couple of the incidents were non-events that didn't change the dynamic of their relationship or push the story to a new height. You need to make these occurrences more extreme to heighten the drama – you're still writing a little conservatively. Use your imagination a bit more.

I also think the ending still needs work. At the moment, it doesn't pay off on the story you've built up. It lacks real incident or punch, since when I got there, I didn't feel there was a proper climax to Jimmy's illness and his relationship with Olivia. You need to finish on a bang – leave the reader wanting more.

Keep at it, Danny. You have a great product here, but it still needs more work to reach its full potential.

Good luck,

Nick.

The first thing I felt when I read Nick's review was shock, since I'd been hoping that I'd fixed the problems he'd identified with the previous draft. As it turned out though, my novel was nowhere near as developed as I'd thought, and as the shock wore off, all the anxiety, all the fear that I'd felt the previous night tightened its grip around my throat, and I was once again strangled with a flurry of doubt.

Was I an idiot for bailing on such a safe, lucrative career?

Did I really make the right decision?

Was I wrong in thinking that I'm good enough to make it as an author?

I tried to fight the onslaught of questions but they kept on coming as my anxiety, my fear, grew stronger and stronger. I tried to picture myself achieving my dream: I tried to envision a huge teary smile spread across my face in the moment of being offered a publishing contract; and I tried to envision myself as a happy 40 year old – as a successful author surrounded by a loving, supportive family. But just like the previous night, the picture was a blur. Every day it seemed less and less attainable, and the image of that lonely, unfulfilled, miserable man became more and more vivid in its place.

The next day

A few years beforehand, the fear that I was feeling then would've plunged me into an alcohol-fuelled tailspin. It would've plummeted me into a ghastly depression – one that would've been so acute it would've almost certainly culminated in another trip to the psych ward. Then again, maybe even that's giving myself too much credit, since a few years beforehand, I would've never had the courage to take the risk that I was taking then. When I began university, my self-worth was predicated on being a scholarship-holding Commerce/Law student, destined to have a mansion on the harbour, to drive a sports car, and to take my future wife and kids overseas every year. There was no way in hell I could've ever given that up.

But, I'd come a long way since then. By 2012, not only could I take that fear on, but through all the therapy and self-analysis I'd done, I also had the psychological skillset to be able to stare it down and stop it from crippling me. To once again use my war metaphor, I now had enough men guarding my fortress to prevent depression's army from re-attacking my brain.

So after breakfast the next day, I sat down comfortably on my bed, and took a long, deep breath. I continued breathing, in ... and out ... in ... and out, gradually calming myself down as I reminded myself of the premise upon which I based my confidence – of the reason why I believed I'd be able to make it as an author.

I have the right attitude to succeed, I said out loud. *I'm so determined, so self-motivated, so disciplined; and I'll never, ever,* ever *quit. With this attitude, it's only a matter of time before I produce a novel that's ready to be published, and after that, I trust God that I'll get the break I need to achieve my dream.*

Working at the call centre and then getting a disappointing book review has made me lose sight of this lately, and that's what's allowed all this fear to shoot through. And from time to time, that's going to happen. I'm travelling a difficult road, and I'm going to have setbacks. There are going to be times when I feel scared. There are going to be times when the future I want doesn't seem possible. But whenever that happens, I need to remind myself that I've got everything it takes to achieve my dream. I need to remember to have faith in myself, to have faith in God, and I need to remember that as long as I do, I can make it come true.

I spent all day on my bed, repeating the same sentiments over and over and over again. And gradually, my fear began to fade. My confidence started to return. And even though I was in the exact same position I was in 24 hours previously, by the end of the day, I felt refortified. I felt optimistic. I felt ready for the challenge.

I'm going to do this! I told myself. *I don't know when it's going to happen, but sooner or later, I'm going to achieve my dream!*

Once again, I tried to picture myself in the moment of being offered a publishing contract, with a huge smile spread across my face and tears of joy streaming down my cheeks – where I'm so suffused with happiness that I can't even talk.

For the first time since I'd started working at the call centre, it felt real, again.

In its first six months of operation, Open Skies raised over $13,500 for the greenhouses project in Peru, and started funding the women's centre project in Cambodia too. I was really happy with our progress, and it felt great to finally be helping people after spending two years setting the organisation up. Raising nearly $15,000 in total during our first few months was a really good effort, and we knew it would go a long way to assisting those in need.

Succeeding with Open Skies also gave me an extra shot in the arm of confidence to succeed with my writing. It reinforced the idea that if I worked hard and believed in myself, then I really could achieve what I was going for. Not a day went by where I wouldn't picture my deliriously overjoyed self in the moment of being offered a publishing contract, and I knew that I could be that person if I just kept having faith.

And at some point in May, that was the message I got tattooed across my arm:

Faith Conquers.

*

Towards the end of the month, I also saw my psychologist for my regular check-up.

'How've you been going, Danny?' Dr Gregor asked.

'Pretty well on the whole,' I said. 'I quit my job at the call centre, and I'm back to writing full-time again. I'm really enjoying it, and most of the time, I'm confident I'll succeed.'

We kept on talking.

'Do you still get days when you feel scared, though?' he asked. 'Do you still get days when you feel terrified that you're never going to get your novel published and that you'll end up a broke, lonely, miserable 40 year old?'

I nodded solemnly.

'Yeah. Sometimes.'

We explored the issue further before Dr Gregor offered me a piece of advice.

'I think you need to focus more on the journey you're on, and less on the end outcome,' he said. 'It's going to be a while before your novel is completely finished and ready to try and publish, so there's no need to think about what's going to happen then until the moment's upon you. Right now, it's better to just enjoy yourself. After all, you're writing full-time – right now, you're *already* living your dream! So experience it to the full. Be wholly present in the moment. Enjoy it for what it is instead of fretting about whether or not you'll get published and what may or may not happen if you don't. Whenever you do stress about all of that, you're only taking away from your enjoyment of this exciting journey that you're embarking upon. Later on, if you do end up getting rejected by every agent and publisher in the business, you can worry. But right now – just forget about it.'

July, 2012

My novel still wasn't published; I was still flat broke; I still didn't have a girlfriend; I was still living with my parents; and all those scholarship holders that I used to beat my brains out competing with back in the day had expense accounts and were getting paid $100,000 salaries, while I barely scraped by tutoring high school and uni students.

But ever since I started living more in the present and enjoying my journey for what it was, I was the happiest I'd been since the scholarship dinner at the start of university.

The Bhagavad Gita, an ancient Indian Yogic scripture, says that it is better to live your own destiny imperfectly than to live an imitation of somebody else's life with perfection. And, as imperfect as it may have seemed, I could definitely say that I was living my destiny.

No wonder happiness was seeping back into my life.

October, 2012

On the first Wednesday evening of October, I was peacefully reading a novel on the couch in the kitchen when I heard my phone go off.

It was an email from Nick.

I was confident yet nervous. I really did feel like I'd gotten it right this time. But then again, it wouldn't have been the first time I'd been wrong about that.

I opened the email apprehensively, my whole body tingling with anticipation.

You're nearly there, bar a few final fix-ups.

I released a huge sigh of relief. I'd done it. I'd finally done it. It'd taken me six long, hard years, but at last I'd produced a novel that was (nearly) ready to be published. I was thrilled. Completely over the moon. My dream felt so close. So close that I could almost taste it.

November, 2012

It's time I told you how I came up with the idea for the Depression Is Not Destiny Campaign.

In August, I started watching *The X Factor*, which for those who don't know is an amateur singing competition were thousands of people across the country battle it out for a record deal. I was only peripherally interested at first, but I got really hooked when I heard the story of one of the contestants, Samantha Jade. When she was 15, she got signed by Jive Records in the States, the same label as Britney Spears, Pink and Justin Timberlake. She too seemed on her way to stardom, but unfortunately things didn't quite pan out for her and after several years of setbacks, she left the singing industry. Before she auditioned for *The X Factor* in the "Over 25s" category, Sammi was working in a factory counting stock.

'I see this as my last chance for music,' she said at her audition.

I was drawn to her right away. Although our plights had been far from similar, I felt like I could really relate to her struggle – that of having a dream you put your soul into and going through hell to try and make it come true. Knowing how it feels to want something that much, whenever I'd hear her sing, all I could think was, *she is so talented. It is a joy to watch her perform. She more than anyone deserves to have her dream come true.* I'd think the same thing when I was at work, too – coincidentally at that point in time at a factory as well: *she deserves to be on the radio I'm listening to at the moment, she deserves to be on stage at her own concert – not counting stock in a factory like this.* I just wanted the best for her. I really wanted to see her succeed.

Sammi made it through to the Top 12, from which point the artists were to sing a song each week and get eliminated one by one until only the winner was left standing. For her debut, Sammi sung *Wide Awake*, which judge Ronan Keating said she sung better than Katy Perry had sung the original. But unfortunately, the public voted her into the bottom two, and it was only by the judges' vote that she got through to the next round.

Over the next few weeks I thought Sammi was magnificent – I couldn't take my eyes off her when she was on stage, and the song she'd sing would often be stuck in my head for the rest of the night. But in the fifth and seventh rounds she found herself in the bottom two again, each time just scraping through to see another day. She admitted that coming so close to being eliminated had left her feeling "very defeated", particularly since she'd had a history of setbacks and as a result of which, was already low on confidence. Testing her resolve further still was all the unwarranted hate she was receiving over social media, saying that she couldn't sing and was only on the show because she was friends with judge Guy Sebastian; the vitriol was so intense that she was even receiving death threats. It was a time when a lot of people would've collapsed and folded, but being the fighter Sammi is she kept soldiering on, kept listening to the judges and trying to get better.

'You're a great singer, but you need to connect with the viewers more,' they said. 'You need to show your personality more. You need to be a little edgier.'

She took it all on, and as the competition progressed she went from strength to strength, and Australia got to realise how nice, how genuine, how truly loveable she really was. Her confidence seemed to gradually come back, and from the semi-finals on there was no stopping her – she was absolutely spellbinding – and in late November, Australia voted her the winner. In that moment, the emotion in her face was haunting, one of the most beautiful expressions of joy I've ever seen in my life. I literally had goose bumps just looking at her. As an artist I was deeply inspired by her triumph after everything she'd been through, and as a person I was flushed with pure and utter happiness for her. It couldn't have happened to a more deserving girl, and I'm really glad I was there to witness it.

After the finale, I found myself musing about *The X Factor* in general:

It's obviously great for Sammi and the other top contestants who'll surely go on to get record deals, but to say that it only benefits the singers isn't doing it justice. On top of being a talent show, The X Factor *is a treasure trove of uplifting individual tales that transcend all realms of life, and by providing a forum for the contestants to tell their story, and for the country to then be able to follow their journey and watch them beat their demons and succeed,* The X Factor *gives hope and inspiration to viewers who need it.*

Thinking about *The X Factor* in that way then got me thinking about my own story:

If people currently suffering from depression knew what I went through and then saw me in my ardently happy moment when I've achieved my dream, then wouldn't they be inspired too? Wouldn't it give them hope that they could also recover and go on to live a happy, healthy life?

And so, the Depression Is Not Destiny Campaign was born.

EPILOGUE

I never thought the first few years of my adulthood would turn out the way they have. When I was 18 at the scholarship dinner, I was sure that I'd finish my Commerce/Law degree and by now be making six figures at a management consulting firm or an investment bank. Never did I think I'd fall victim to depression, become an alcoholic, found a charity, develop bipolar disorder from a doctor's negligence, go to a psych ward, write a second book, quit law, return to the psych ward, un-enrol from honours and at 24 end up a philanthropist, a mental health advocate and an aspiring author who's still broke and living with his parents. It's been a strange ride, and at times an extremely painful one, but the truth is that I wouldn't change any of it, because it's brought me to the wonderful place that I'm in right now: I'm helping impoverished communities through my foundation; I'm about to launch a mental health campaign that I hope will inspire thousands of people; and with a bit of luck, I'll soon achieve my dream of becoming a published author. Above all else, however, I am finally happy, and I can't ask for anything more than that. At last, I have enough armed men stationed outside my fortress to prevent depression's army from being able to get through again. It still tries to – I'm often getting tested by the inevitable frustrations and disappointments of life – but I now understand myself so well and my coping mechanisms are so refined that these days, I can handle all the tribulations that used to rip me to shreds.

'How did you recover?' is the most common question I'm asked.

I get the feeling that half the time the person's expecting me to have some wild, crazy explanation they've never heard of before, as if how to beat depression is one of the eternal mysteries of life. But at the end of the day, how I recovered was very simple: I never gave up on happiness, I never stopped fighting my illness, and most importantly, I got the help I so desperately needed. And if I had to identify the biggest problem surrounding the mental health industry right now, I'd probably say that it's the fact that so many sufferers fail to seek help. In all my interaction with victims in group therapy sessions, psych wards, mental health forums, charity functions and even in day to day life, I've heard a million and one reasons for why people don't get help. Sometimes it's financial, which is tragic (and even then there are alternatives), but often money's got nothing to do with it.

A lot of the time it's stigma:

'If I see a psychologist, take medication or read self-help books, then people might judge me – so no way!'

Nearly as often it's pride:

'I refuse to "get help" because I want to sort my problems out for myself. "Getting help" is weak, and if I "got help", then I'd feel like a failure.'

And of course there's also fear – of facing your demons, of going down a path unknown.

It's hard for me to relate to such lines of thinking, because I never had any of these hang-ups. I just wanted to get well again – plain and simple. If that meant seeing a psychologist, then I saw a psychologist. If that meant taking medication, then I took medication. If that meant checking into a psych ward, then I checked into a psych ward. Stigma, pride and fear never came into it – and logically speaking, it shouldn't for anyone else either. As many professionals in the field say:

'If you had a broken leg, would you get help?

If you had diabetes, would you get help?

If you had cancer, would you get help?

Of course you would.

So you need to get help if you have a mental illness, too.'

So if there's one thing I can say to the 350 million people on this planet that are estimated to have depression – and to everyone else who suffers from another form of mental illness – it is that: abandon all your hang-ups and get the help you need. I did, and it saved my life. And it can save yours, too.

Yet in saying that, I also understand that I was extremely fortunate to receive the treatment I did. My parents were very supportive from day one, and could afford to pay for my medical and psychological bills. And when I think of my experience with mental illness as a whole, it's this good fortune that really comes to mind. To the best of my recollection, at no point did I ever think of myself as unlucky for having suffered so severely. Quite the opposite – I've always thought of myself as extremely blessed to have received the help I did to beat my illness. And it's this good fortune that's motivated me to start the Depression Is Not Destiny Campaign.

'Aren't you going to find it hard?' my mum often asks. 'You'll be spilling your soul to the entire world. You'll be opening yourself up for everyone to see some of the most private, intimate moments of your life. Not to mention that mental illness still carries such a stigma – by being so open about your experiences with it, you're going to cop all sorts of criticism from all the ignorant Tom, Dick and Harrys out there. Hell, Samantha Jade was receiving death threats, and what you're doing is more controversial than singing! I do think you have the chance to help a lot of people, but you're also exposing yourself to a hell of a lot of abuse from any person with internet access.'

She's right – I'm sure I will find it hard at times. Contrary to how it may appear, I'm actually a very private person. Aside from Sylvia back in 2008 and 2009, I've hardly discussed my struggles with anyone except for my family and my medical team. Even my closest friends have no idea what I've been through – they'll read this book and be shocked as hell. So

I'm sure I will find being so open quite challenging. But that doesn't mean that I'm going to let it stop me.

'You're right, Mum,' I always reply. 'But I'll take that on. The way I see it, if it wasn't for the support you and Dad have given me and for all the treatment I've received, I have no idea where I'd be right now. Maybe I'd be in a psych ward. Maybe I'd be homeless. Maybe I'd be dead. So the way I see it, I'm lucky just to be here. I'm really, really lucky just to be here. So if there's anything I can do to help someone who's in the same position I was in – particularly someone who isn't as fortunate to receive the help that I got – then I'm sure as hell going to do it.'

As Mr Williams once said to me:

'To whom much is given, much is expected.'

Also by Danny Baker ...

I Will Not Kill Myself, Olivia

First love never dies, but can depression bury it alive?

Jimmy Wharton's good-looking, popular and studies commerce/law at Sydney's best university. Everything points to him having a wonderful life, but in reality, he's crippled with a debilitating case of depression – one that he feels so suffocated by that he starts to believe that suicide is his only way out.

However, he knows that killing himself would absolutely shatter his high school sweetheart Olivia. So instead of doing so, he promises her that he'll get the help he needs, and in return, she vows to support him in every way she can. But finding that light at the end of the tunnel proves to be the most challenging, tumultuous, heartbreaking thing either of them have ever had to do. And, just when it looks like they've glued their hearts back together again and finally found it, Jimmy's illness brings him face to face with death.

And in a bizarre twist, also puts Olivia's life at risk too.

You'll find this book appealing if:

- You enjoyed Danny Baker's novel *Anxious in Love.*

- You're a fan of gritty, passionate love stories that build towards a climactic, heart-pounding finish.

- You want to relive the highs, the lows and the intoxicating rush that's unique to first love.

- You're a young adult who wants to read about another young adult striving for the same things you are.

- You're interested in understanding depression better; you suffer from depression yourself and you want to feel like you're not alone; or you want to see how you can better support a loved one with depression.

- You're a parent of a young adult and you want to understand how easily your child can tumble into depression, and you want to prepare yourself to be able to recognise the symptoms if they ever do fall victim (unfortunately, depression strikes as many as 20% of teens, and for 15-24 year olds, suicide is the third, the second and the leading cause of death in the US, the UK and Australia, respectively).

You're unlikely to enjoy this book if:

- You despise swearing.

- You are put off by explicit sex scenes.

- You're after a light-hearted story.

Editorial Reviews

"Centred around Jimmy and Olivia's heartfelt, passionate and troubled love, I WILL NOT KILL MYSELF, OLIVIA is a painfully honest, authentic and provocative novel ... one that presents a mesmerising portrayal of the all-consuming force of depression that dominates the main character ... one that takes the reader on a highly emotional journey ... and one that achieves a perfect balance

of emotions, action and drama." **The Columbia Review**

"A modern day Romeo and Juliet - a powerful, heart-wrenching story that takes you on an emotional rollercoaster ride as Jimmy and Olivia try to hang on desperately to love in the face of Jimmy's mounting depression." **Nick Bleszynski, bestselling author**

"An explicitly realistic, absolutely intriguing and stunningly gritty novel ... one that snatches the reader's attention right from the start ... and one that provides fantastic food for thought for all young adults." **Pacific Book Review**

"A romance story that tugs at the heart, and entices readers with pure raw emotion ... from steamy, unadulterated throes of passion to being tossed into the deepest, darkest depths of despair, Baker creates an immersive world for Jimmy and Olivia ... you will feel their love, experience their torment, and empathize with their pain." **San Diego Book Review**

"One of the most singularly powerful books about depression on the market." **Midwest Book Review**.